50 GREATS POOLE PIRATES

50 GREATS

POOLE PIRATES

ROBERT BAMFORD & GLYNN SHAILES

TEMPUS

Frontispiece: Warming up in the pits.

First published 2004

Tempus Publishing Limited
The Mill, Brimscombe Port,
Stroud, Gloucestershire, GL5 2QG
www.tempus-publishing.com

© Robert Bamford and Glynn Shailes, 2004

The right of Robert Bamford and Glynn Shailes to be identified
as the Authors of this work has been asserted in accordance with
the Copyrights, Designs and Patents Act 1988.

British Library Cataloguing in Publication Data.
A catalogue record for this book is available from the British Library.

ISBN 0 7524 3257 5

Typesetting and origination by Tempus Publishing Limited
Printed and bound in Great Britain

Foreword by Alun Rossiter

I thought it was a great idea when I heard that Robert Bamford and Glynn Shailes were producing a book on 50 greats of Poole Speedway. I was even more delighted upon learning I was to be included in the elite bunch! Indeed, I consider Poole to be the Manchester United of the speedway world, with all the other clubs striving to match the achievements of the Pirates. Certainly, the Dorset side enjoys great support, and over the years the Pirates have claimed much on-track success. As a rider, I was always happy in my spells with the club, riding under the management of Mervyn Stewkesbury and Pete Ansell. Nowadays, the Pirates are still in great hands of course, under the diligent promotion of Matt Ford and Mike Golding.

During my time in the saddle, I was proud to be part of the side that won the National League Championship in 1989, riding alongside the likes of Craig Boyce, Leigh Adams, Alastair Stevens, Gary Allan, Tony Langdon and Kevin Smart. During that year, I particularly remember the matches against Wimbledon, who at the time were under the promotion of Russell Lanning. The two sides were always so pumped up for these meetings and both sets of fans created a wonderful atmosphere. There was one major disappointment in 1989 though, and that was the final of the Knock-Out Cup, when we lost out to Berwick. The Bandits battled hard in the first leg at Wimborne Road and around their own patch at Berrington Lough; they had so much home track advantage we just couldn't contain them.

Things went even better for Poole in 1990, however, when we not only retained the league title but also won the Knock-Out Cup, defeating Middlesbrough in the final to complete a glorious double. The backbone of the team was much the same that year, although three changes saw Tom Knudsen, Rod Colquhoun and Gary Chessell replace Leigh Adams, Kevin Smart and Alastair Stevens.

Another year I remember fondly is 1994, when, as a Division One side, we stormed to the League Championship, finishing 15 points ahead of runners-up Eastbourne. The team didn't have a weak link and it was a privilege for me to ride with Jason Crump, Craig Boyce, Lars Gunnestad, Steve Schofield, Jorgen Johansson and Steve Masters. I especially recall the Four-Team Championship final at Peterborough that year, when Lars Gunnestad had to drop out and I was called up to replace him in the meeting. Lars had been riding brilliantly all season, but I was delighted to score 6 points from 3 starts to help the Pirates take the silverware ahead of Cradley Heath, Eastbourne and Coventry.

Poole is a traditional speedway town and the club has a marvellous history. I trust that in reading this book it will bring back many happy memories for all supporters of the Skull and Crossbones.

Alun Rossiter, former skipper of the Pirates
June 2004

Acknowledgements

As ever, the amazing John Jarvis has provided the answers to numerous questions at the drop of a hat. Acknowledgement is also made to Oxford-based Poole supporter Chris Broadway, whose wonderful collection of Pirates memorabilia has always been made available to us. It was reassuring to know the answers to many queries were no more than a telephone call away. We would also like to thank Chris for his encouragement and also for a number of helpful suggestions in the compilation of this publication. Grateful thanks are due to Norman Young, known as 'Tich', who has been at Poole Speedway from day one. Tich was the machine examiner for many years and can still be found working in the pits on race nights, helping with the smooth running of meetings. His excellent memory of so many happenings at Wimborne Road has proved of great value to us on many occasions. Old friend Keith Farman was, as ever, a source of intriguing snippets of information, and for that we offer much gratitude. Matt Jackson was also extremely helpful with information from his vast database on various riders' dates and places of birth.

The speedway press has been a constant source of information over the years and to this end, we would like to express our gratitude to various magazines, namely *Speedway World*, *Speedway Echo*, *Speedway News*, *Speedway Star*, *On The Track*, *The Motor Cycle* and *Broadsider*. Mention must also be made here of the excellent series of *Speedway Archives* publications by Peter Jackson, which have proved to be an invaluable point of reference. As ever, no book would be complete without photographs and, to this end, the authors acknowledge the excellent images from F. Fowler, Wright Wood, J.P.B. Shelley, Stan Vicars, Ralph Jackson, C.F. Wallace, T.H. Everitt, Howard G. Murphy, Alf Weedon, Phil Hilton, Bernard Crapper, Dave Payne, Alan Whale, Les Aubrey and www.mike-patrick.com, plus the wonderful collections of Geoff Parker, Pete Ross and Chris Broadway.

Many, many thanks to one and all.

Robert Bamford and Glynn Shailes

Note on Statistics

Please note that all statistics are complete up to 28 April 2004, when Tony Rickardsson rode his final match for the Pirates, having decided to call it a day with the domestic British scene. The figures contained herein refer only to meetings ridden for Poole in the UK, as it has proved impossible to trace full details of the Pirates' various tours of Sweden (1948, 1953 and 1955) and Poland (1959 and 1969). To give a complete picture of each rider's record with the club, all appearances as a guest are included in the statistics. I have attempted to separate the statistics into the most important categories, i.e. League and National Trophy/Knock-Out Cup, while the line entitled 'Others' refers to challenge matches and various cup competitions, including Anniversary Cup, Hants & Dorset Trophy, Autumn Cup, Festival of Britain Trophy, Queen's Cup, Southern Shield, Inter-Divisional Tournament, Britannia Shield, Easter Cup, Western Cup, Charles Knott Trophy, Spring Gold Cup, Champagne Stakes, League Cup, Southern Cup, National Series, Premiership, BSPA Cup, Craven Shield, British League Cup, Play-Offs etc. That leaves the various three- and four-team tournaments and, as shown, these have all been added together for their own total. The Craven Shield finals of 2000-2002 are included as three-team tournaments, since that is the format they were staged under.

Robert Bamford

Introduction

Poole Speedway is a very special club within the sport and has always been so. I would say Poole is one of the few speedway towns, if not the only one, in this country. Talk to any supporter of years ago and sooner or later Poole Speedway and the achievements of the team will most surely crop up. I recall the days of three divisions when the Pirates went from the Third to the Second Division and, in 1956, to the First Division. All this was done through the proper route, by winning the league title and thus gaining promotion as a result of the riders' on-track efforts.

Throughout their long and distinguished time in the sport, Poole have had their ups and downs, but have always bounced back, and invariably been stronger than ever. I believe tradition means much to the supporters of Poole – I've found them to be loyal to their club, but never afraid to speak their minds should something not be right. I believe also that Poole fans are always happiest when they have local folk, who they can relate to, running the club. It's mostly been that way since 1948 and over the years I have always managed to make at least one visit to Wimborne Road per season. I particularly remember telling my father after a visit in 1948 that 'they cheer the opposition there as well as their own men, Dad', and they are still doing so in 2004. I was fortunate enough to retire from work early, whereupon the first thing I did was to purchase a season ticket to watch the Pirates in action, and that happy situation has been going on for some five years now.

It is good also to meet so many Poole fans who have supported their club over the years and to relive with them many outstanding memories. Among these is the occasion in 1952 when, as a Second Division side, the Pirates met top-flight New Cross in the National Trophy. On 23 July the Poole boys visited the 'Frying Pan' home of the Rangers for the first leg and lost heavily by 75 points to 33. Nobody really gave the Dorseteers much chance in the return match, but in a meeting that had every Poole supporter on their toes, the Pirates set about New Cross with vigour and all but made up the deficit, winning the second leg 72-36. Amazingly, they very nearly made up the 42 points they were in arrears from the first leg, and had Terry Small not crashed in the final race then Poole could possibly have won on aggregate. Going back a little further, I also recall the England 'C' Test matches in 1951, when the car parks were packed with supporters who couldn't get into the stadium but were happy to listen to announcer Cliff Cooper giving out the results over the public address system.

This book has been a labour of love and profiles 50 great Poole riders, with relevant photographs and statistics. It is not necessarily the greatest 50 Poole riders: in my view all speedway riders are great. I would like to thank my friend Chris Broadway who, although Oxford-based, is a long-time supporter of the Pirates. He has been a constant source of encouragement and has always been available to help iron out various queries on heat details, etc. I would also like to thank Norman Young, who still helps in the Poole pits and has answered many of my questions. There are many other good folk whose advice and help I have valued, so warm thanks to you all.

So please enjoy what Robert Bamford and I are proud to call a very good read. If you do, our efforts have been very worthwhile indeed. Oh, and for those fans who have asked who my favourite Pirates were, I can tell you there are three of them, namely Bill Holden, plus the 'Me and My Shadow' pair of Ken Middleditch and Tony Lewis. The latterly mentioned duos team riding was something extra-special, as every old-time supporter will confirm. Believe me, there is nothing quite like it in speedway today.

Talking of today, although there have been structural changes, as well as alterations in personnel, riders, bikes and the track surface, the one thing that hasn't changed, and I'm sure never will, is the buzz you get when entering the stadium. Just stand for a minute before any meeting commences and you will understand what I mean. As I've already mentioned, the opposition will be applauded as much in 2004 as they were when things began way back in 1948.

Glynn Shailes

50 Poole Pirates Greats

Leigh Adams
Bill Andrew
Scott Autrey
Jack Biggs
David Biles
Joe Bowkis
Craig Boyce
Alan Chambers
Marvyn Cox
Bruce Cribb
Brian Crutcher
John Davis
Reidar Eide
Sam Ermolenko
Odd Fossengen
Ronnie Genz
Ross Gilbertson

Colin Gooddy
Lars Gunnestad
Gary Havelock
Charlie Hayden
Sid Hazzard
Frank Holcombe
Bill Holden
Dick Howard
Ticker James
Allan Kidd
Michael Lee
Tony Lewis
Christer Lofqvist
Mark Loram
Ken Middleditch
Neil Middleditch
Geoff Mudge

Gote Nordin
Fred Pawson
Ron Preston
Cyril Quick
Tony Rickardsson
Alun Rossiter
Steve Schofield
Malcolm Simmons
Christer Sjosten
Terry Small
Kevin Smith
Pete Smith
Jimmy Squibb
Norman Strachan
Johnny Thomson
Martin Yeates

Born: 28 April 1971, Mildura, Victoria, Australia

Competition	Matches	Points
League	62	685
Knock-Out Cup	12	142
Others	18	199
Three- and four-team tournaments	6	26
Pirates total	**98**	**1,052**

Leigh Scott Adams first rode in junior speedway at the age of just nine. He developed into a young man of exceptional talent at his chosen discipline and this was spotted by former rider Neil Street, who recommended him to Poole where he was at the time team manager. This was in 1988, and later on that season Leigh came over to the UK on what could rightly be described as a 'working holiday'. He duly rode in 4 matches for Poole in the National Junior League, the first of which was at Arena-Essex on 20 August. At once Leigh revealed his potential to score 6 points and he was to average exactly 9.00 from his holiday stint.

He returned to Britain in 1989 and National League racing with Poole, where he linked in with a Pirates side that included two other Aussie boys, Craig Boyce and Tony Langdon. In the beginning he was included in the team at reserve, although there was no doubting he was more than capable of holding down a spot in the main body of the side. However, the speedway rules at the time meant that as he hadn't ridden in the league before he would have an assessed average of 2.00, hence his reserve berth position.

Straight away Leigh showed what a nonsense this was, making a storybook debut as he raced to a paid maximum (14+1 points) against Exeter in an Easter Trophy match at Wimborne Road on 24 March. After that the big scores simply flowed from his wheels, with 13+1 points at Ipswich in Poole's first league match of the campaign on 13 April, followed by 9+3 points (paid maximum) at Mildenhall six days later.

The Pirates looked awesome as they won their first 6 league matches on the trot and

their new Australian recruit was most certainly playing his part. Week by week at Wimborne Road he showed that he was more than equal to the challenge of National League racing and on the team's travels he took all the different tracks in his stride. This and the form of his team-mates saw the Dorset side go on to take the Championship by 5 clear points from Wimbledon, with Adams posting a fabulous 9.19 average from a full quota of 34 league matches, having netted a total of 362 points and 6 maximums (3 full and 3 paid).

In the Knock-Out Cup, the Pirates saw off Hackney, Eastbourne and Wimbledon to reach the final, but after defeating Berwick 50-46 in the first leg at home they went down to a 63-33 loss in the return match at Berrington Lough. Leigh contributed tallies of 14 and 12 points respectively, but only his skipper Alun Rossiter was able to back him with anything like normal form in the second leg against a determined Bandits outfit.

To further his career, the Australian then moved up a league to join Swindon for a large fee, rumoured to be £20,000-plus, in time for the 1990 season.

His debut for the Robins subsequently occurred in a Gold Cup match against Oxford at Blunsdon on 24 March, when he netted 8+2 points. Leigh's armchair style of riding quickly made him a firm favourite with the Swindon fans and he went on to achieve a satisfactory 6.81 league average in his first year of Division One racing. The following season that figure increased to 8.48 and he was a shining light in a Robins side that ended the term as holders of the unwanted wooden spoon. Only the late decision of Mildenhall to return to racing in Division Two after a couple of years out of the sport actually saved Swindon from being relegated.

When 1992 came along Adams established himself as a heat-leader, recording 298 points for a league average of 9.55. Unhappily for the Robins, they again propped up the final table

and the ignominy of relegation was unavoidable. However, it was a successful year for Leigh personally as he won his first Australian national title and in addition captured the World Under-21 Championship after beating Mark Loram in a run-off at Pfaffenhofen, Germany, on 23 August. With Swindon dropping down a division he was forced to seek pastures new and duly joined Arena-Essex, where he was to spend three seasons (1993-1995), during which he registered a staggering total of 1,435 points from 109 league matches.

With Hackney returning to domestic racing under the guise of London for 1996, a change of scenery saw Leigh hit a 10.12 average for the Lions. Sadly, the venture only lasted for that one year before again closing and the Aussie was back at Swindon in 1997, when the Robins became founder members of the newly-formed Elite League. He enjoyed a fine return to the Blunsdon set-up too, plundering 444 league points for an average of 9.96 and helping his side to a creditable third-place finish. Leigh's average dipped a tad to 8.95 in 1998, but little did anyone know at the season's end that it was to be the last season of top-flight racing at Blunsdon. A riders' pay policy was introduced and the top Elite League boys could not accept the money on offer, and eventually Swindon applied to race in the Premier League in 1999. Adams found himself without a track for some time until King's Lynn brought him in from the cold at the end of April that year. He wasted little time in hitting the high scores and ended the season with a league average of 9.48 for the Knights, but better was to come in 2000 when he accumulated 396 points for an average of 10.24 and occupied top spot in the overall Elite League figures.

In 2001, the man from Mildura joined Oxford, and this surprised many folk who thought the Sandy Lane circuit wasn't the type of track where he could maintain the high standards he had set for himself. Leigh soon blew this theory to smithereens, however, by becoming the Cheetahs' leading rider and, with a haul of 411 points, he played an important role in helping the side to League Championship glory. Another 444 points were accrued as he remained on board in 2002, a year which also saw him help Australia to retain the Speedway World Cup they had won the previous year at Wroclaw in Poland. The British-based 2002 competition represented Leigh's third triumph with Australia as they had also taken victory in the 1999 World Team Cup final at Pardubice in the Czech Republic.

At the end of 2002, the future of Oxford in the higher sphere of British racing looked to be in serious doubt and for Adams the wheel of fortune turned full circle when he returned to Poole. His on-track performances demonstrated that he was pleased to be back with the Dorset club, and along with multi-World Champion Tony Rickardsson, the pair formed a powerful spearhead. The Pirates totally dominated the 2003 season, finishing top of the Elite League table by an 8-point margin and then claiming the Championship, courtesy of a Play-Off victory over Coventry. The ever-consistent Australian headed the club's league scoring with 316 points and an average of 9.97 from 27 matches, whilst also compiling 6 maximums (4 full and 2 paid). Capping a marvellous campaign, the Pirates then completed a glorious treble by defeating Coventry (again) to win the Knock-Out Cup, before beating Eastbourne to lift the British League Cup. Poole fans could certainly be forgiven for thinking Adams had the Midas touch, for in his two seasons with the club he helped them to win no fewer than four trophies! Still being a Swindon asset, Leigh was awarded a much-deserved Testimonial in 2003, and his special meeting went ahead at Blunsdon on 31 July, when a packed audience paid tribute to one of the legends of the modern era. A first-class line-up was assembled for the individual event and fittingly it was Adams himself who won the final, beating Jason Lyons, Joe Screen and Travis McGowan. In 2004 Leigh retraced the path of his early career when, upon Swindon rejoining the Elite League, he once again agreed to don the famous Robins race-jacket.

On the individual front, Adams made his one and only appearance in the old one-off World Final at Pocking, Germany in 1993, when he recorded a 4-point tally. He has of course been a regular in the Grand Prix series since 1996, the highlights being victories in the 2002 Scandinavian GP at the Ullevi Stadium, Gothenburg, the 2003 Slovenian GP at the Matije Gubca Stadium, Krsko, and the 2004 Swedish GP at the Olympic Stadium, Stockholm. Overall, his best efforts were fourth place in both 2002 and 2003, when he ended the series with points totals of 127 and 126 respectively. Meanwhile, in his own back yard, Leigh has added to his Australian Championship victory in 1992, with further title successes in 1993, 1994, 1997, 2000, 2002 and 2003.

Born: 13 December 1940, Palmerston North, New Zealand

Competition	Matches	Points
League	86	779
Knock-Out Cup	5	55
Others	12	110
Four-team tournaments	1	9
Pirates total	**104**	**953**

Aside from riding a speedway bike with great proficiency, Bill was also well known as a professional jockey, competing under the name of E.C. Andrew (his full name actually being Errol Carroll Andrew). Looking at his career in the shale game, he initially came over to the UK to ride for Newcastle in 1962, the Diamonds at the time being members of the Provincial League. The sport was really taking off again in the north-east and Newcastle's go-ahead promoter Mike Parker was determined to build a good side, having reopened the Brough Park doors to the sport the previous season. There is no doubting that he signed a winner in the young Bill, and the Kiwi quickly settled down to become a sound scorer, backing the efforts of the club's skipper and leading rider Brian Craven. In what was personally a fine campaign, his 'never give up' style of riding won him many admirers and his final league tally of 155½ points saw him end as runner-up in the team's scoring behind his captain.

His good form was recognised internationally as the season drew to a close, when he was selected to ride for the Overseas in a Test series against Great Britain. Andrew was to appear in 4 of the 5 matches, netting a total of 13 points, his highest score being 7 in the first Test at Poole on 12 September, which the Overseas won 56-52. Great Britain came back to register a 3-2 success in the series, but it was

the experience gained that was the most important matter for 'Battling' Bill Andrew. The New Zealander also bagged 29 points from three qualifying rounds in the Provincial Riders' Championship, making it through to the final at Belle Vue on 22 September, when he recorded 5 points. It was a shock to all Newcastle supporters when he didn't return to these shores for the 1963 season, but Mike Parker made another important signing from New Zealand when he managed to get a certain Ivan Mauger to put pen to paper.

However, in 1964, the year in which the Provincial League promoters rode 'black', outside the jurisdiction of the Speedway Control Board, Andrew returned to British speedway and once again linked with the Diamonds. He quickly showed that a year's absence hadn't dulled his ability as he again finished second in the Newcastle scoring, behind the great Ivan Mauger, with 174 league points. According to the speedway pundits, Bill had returned 'better than ever' and he certainly played a major part as the Diamonds claimed the League Championship by 3 points from Hackney.

During the winter, peace was declared on the speedway front, with the National and Provincial Leagues coming together to form the British League. There had to be an equalisation of team strengths and Bill found himself moved down to the South Coast as a member of the Poole side. It didn't take him long to settle in and he was soon breathing down the neck of another Pirates signing, Ronnie Genz, at the top of the side's averages. An early indication of his brilliance was given on 19 April when Poole journeyed to Exeter for the second leg of the

Easter Trophy. Old-time fans of the Dorset side still talk about Andrew's actions in heat 11 to this very day. Ronnie Genz and Exeter's Colin Gooddy were having a right royal tussle up front, with Bill occupying third spot. After 3 laps Genz edged in front, but was re-passed by Gooddy, only for Andrew to make a superhuman effort on the last bend and, breathtakingly, take the chequered flag from the Falcon.

Although a New Zealander, Bill rode in the qualifying rounds of the World Championship and made it through to the British Final at West Ham on 31 August. Unfortunately, he enjoyed no luck at all on a night when conditions were difficult due to heavy rain, mustering only a single point. During the season Andrew had, like a number of riders, switched to ESO machinery and this equipment could almost have been made for him. One undoubted highlight occurred on 8 September, when his former side, Newcastle, visited Poole for a league match. The Pirates raced to a 45-33 victory, with Bill completing as fine a 12-point maximum as one is likely to witness, his performance including a 10th-heat triumph over compatriot Ivan Mauger.

The 1965 season was a new beginning for speedway in Britain and it could be looked upon as a great success. Poole ended the campaign in a mid-table position (tenth) and their Kiwi acquisition could look back on his own efforts with a good deal of satisfaction. He remained ever-present throughout the side's 34 league matches and accumulated a total of 316 points for a solid average of 8.99 in what was certainly a year to remember. The pint-sized racer also notched 7 full maximums (including the aforementioned one against Newcastle), as well as recommending fellow countryman Bruce Cribb to the Poole management. 'Cribby', of course, was to go on and serve the Pirates with distinction until the end of 1969.

Andrew returned to Wimborne Road in 1966 and again put together a string of tall scores as he battled to be top dog with Ronnie Genz in the club's averages. Having finished as runner-up to 'Genno' the previous year, a reversal of the positions saw Bill take over top spot, with 297 points from 33 matches giving him a league average of 9.29. Three full 12-point maximums were gleaned along the way in home meetings

against King's Lynn, Wolverhampton and Oxford, and he also remained unbeaten when Edinburgh provided the opposition, scoring 11+1 points. On 13 July, Newport travelled to Dorset for a league encounter and a thrilling match ended in a narrow 41-37 win for the Pirates. Andrew had a great night, scorching to an 11-point tally and losing only to stylish Swede Gote Nordin in his first outing. Little did the fans know then, but the following season would see Bill remain in his native land, with his place in the Poole line-up filled by the very same Gote Nordin. Thankfully, the Kiwi wasn't lost to British speedway, or indeed Poole, for he returned to the camp in 1968, and with Nordin and Geoff Mudge as his fellow heat-leaders, the Pirates clearly looked capable of challenging for league honours. Regrettably, things went awry as Nordin quit after just one league match in order to concentrate on business interests in his homeland. Results were poor and Poole slid down the British League table, although Andrew remained a tower of strength at the head of the scoring. The Pirates suffered a real body blow, however, when their main man broke an ankle in his opening ride in the British Final at Wimbledon on 11 July. His injuries were sufficient to put him out of action for the rest of the year and he duly returned to New Zealand to recover. At the time of his misfortune, he had registered 166 points from 19 league matches for an average of 8.34 and it is little wonder that Poole missed his scoring, finishing the season in seventeenth position.

Bill subsequently resumed his British career with Newport in 1970 and he was to spend a couple of years with the Welsh outfit, during which he accrued 512 points from a total of 69 league matches. After completely missing 1972, he spent what turned out to be his final season of domestic racing with Halifax in 1973, when he tallied 167 points from 32 league appearances. Whilst he was a good scorer for both the Wasps and the Dukes, Andrew never really scaled the heights he had in his time at Poole. New Zealand has produced several brilliant riders over the years and Bill was one of them. Although he may not have matched the achievements of Barry Briggs, Ronnie Moore or Ivan Mauger, he was a good team man and a consistent gatherer of points.

Born: 9 July 1953, Maywood, California, USA

Competition	Matches	Points
League	55	460
Knock-Out Cup	5	55
Others	42	397½
Pirates total	102	912½

McKnight and the aforementioned Woods. After linking with Exeter, he quickly became a crowd favourite at the County Ground and, while his compatriots returned home early, Scott enjoyed an excellent first year, scoring 206½ league points for a healthy 6.51 average. There can be little doubt he learned a lot from riding alongside World Champion Ivan Mauger, who joined the Falcons a few weeks into the season after the Rider Control Committee had decreed he should leave Belle Vue.

Things went even better in 1974, when Mauger and Autrey helped Exeter to their first Championship success since 1948. In the process, the American impressively moved his league average up to 8.51, having gleaned 250 race points. After that, he developed into one of the best riders in the world, posting averages in excess of 9.00 for five successive seasons with the Devon outfit, from 1975-1979 inclusive. In fact, his final two years with the Falcons saw his figure rise from 10.59 to 10.91, and having occupied third place in the national figures behind Malcolm Simmons and Ole Olsen in 1978, he joyfully sat at the very top of the pile in 1979.

With Exeter stepping down a league in 1980, it was time for Scott to move on after seven fabulous seasons and a total of 2,058½ league points for the club. He subsequently went to Swindon amid a high level of expectation. The Robins top man Phil Crump wasn't immediately available to start the season, so they desperately needed the services of a classy number one, and in the 'American Express', they clearly had a man with the right pedigree. Following several close calls, he eventually secured his first full maximum for the Robins in a home league match versus Poole on 2 May, when he reeled off 4 straight

Scott Brian Autrey developed a keen interest in motorcycles from the age of eleven and also at one time studied law. However, it was the lure of bikes and a desire to become a speedway rider that put his studies on the 'back burner'. His first skids took place in 1970, and it would be right to say he was a natural. Emphasising this, he went on to finish ninth in the American Championship that year, and in 1971 he moved up to fifth spot. International honours came his way in 1972 when he represented his country against South Africa, and as a measure of his progress, he finished as runner-up to Rick Woods in the USA Final. Autrey represented a new breed of American rider, and in 1973 he arrived in the UK along with fellow countrymen Sumner

victories with consummate ease. The Swindon supporters really appreciated having Autrey on board as he was one of that rare breed of riders who could score equally well at home or away. This was emphasised by double-figure tallies in 7 successive league matches on the road prior to the much-hailed return of Phil Crump in mid-June. Ironically, that coincided with Scott only recording 7+1 points in their initial league match together at Halifax on 21 June, although the two quickly formed a particularly potent spearhead thereafter. The American went on to end the league campaign with a haul of 6 full maximums, not to mention 329 points and a high 9.97 average. Swindon's season ended with a challenge match against local rivals Reading at Blunsdon on 31 October, and although the Robins lost 40-38, the stylish Scott signed off with a 12-point maximum for a weakened septet that had no Phil Crump, no Steve Gresham and no Bob Kilby. It was to be Scott's last appearance for the Robins, as he was transferred to Poole for a reported fee of £16,500 in 1981.

After the season's scheduled opener, a challenge match against Reading, had been rained off, he quickly settled down to life at Wimborne Road. On 1 April, the Pirates belatedly got underway with a League Cup encounter against King's Lynn, and in a hard-fought contest, they just edged home by 48½ points to 47½. Autrey registered 8½ points in the match, the half-point coming as a result of dead-heating with Dave Jessup for third place in heat 4. It wasn't long before double-figure returns became a regular feature of the Poole scorechart, and an early highlight occurred at home on 22 April when he secured a paid maximum (13+2) against former side Swindon in the League Cup. On his travels, there were several notable showings during the league campaign, including 14 points at Coventry, 11 at Belle Vue and 13+1 at Swindon. There were also four-ride full maximums in home matches versus Wimbledon and Leicester, and when Neil Middleditch found the strain of club captaincy too much, it was the ice-cool American who took over, making a fine job of it too! Despite this, and his excellent scoring throughout the British League programme, Scott didn't seem to enjoy the sort of season

his efforts warranted, a fact reflected in the end-of-term league statistics, which showed a total of 256 points and a diminished average of 8.62.

The 1982 season was to be his last in British speedway and he began the League Cup fixtures encouragingly well. He also helped the USA to gain a 3-2 Test series victory over England, although his scoring wasn't consistent, ranging from a single point in matches at Wimbledon and Belle Vue to a tally of 11 at Swindon. In the World Championship, the American Final was held at Long Beach, California, on 12 June, and while Dennis Sigalos secured victory with a fabulous maximum (15), Autrey recorded a score of 13 points to finish level with brothers Shawn and Kelly Moran. He then finished behind the Morans in a run-off, and his fourth position overall was insufficient to earn him a place in the next stage of the competition. With the World Final set to take place on his home soil at the Los Angeles Memorial Coliseum in August, it must have been a bitter disappointment to him. This did in fact manifest itself in his riding, for although he never let Poole down, there was a loss of 'bite' following the meeting at Long Beach. His scoring tapered off and he was unable to rediscover the golden touch, ending the league campaign with a final average of 7.56, having yielded 204 points from 26 matches.

There was one real high spot to remember the year by though, and it was perhaps his finest hour too. The occasion was the World Team Cup Final, staged at London's White City Stadium on 15 August, when Scott was proud to be part of the American team that lifted the prestigious title for the first-ever time. At the end of the season, he called it a day and moved to St Austell for a spell, where he opened an art gallery. He had been a great credit to speedway, his public relations were excellent and he had always conducted himself in a professional manner. Despite missing out on the 1982 World Final, he had at least graced the sport's major event on two occasions, appearing at Katowice, Poland, in 1976, and at Wembley in 1978, his best performance being in the latter event when he finished in third position having recorded 11 points.

Born: 21 March 1922, Melbourne, Victoria, Australia

Competition	Matches	Points
League	49	466
National Trophy	8	89
Others	28	286
Three-team tournaments	1	6
Pirates total	**86**	**847**

Jack Edward Biggs took up speedway in 1945 and subsequently arrived to race in England two years later. He initially thought he would be riding for New Cross, since Clem Mitchell, who had connections with the Old Kent Road club, had made early contact with him. In the event though, Jack signed for Harringay, which in 1947 was a real home from home for Australian riders, with the Racers' side including fellow antipodeans Frank Dolan and the Duggan brothers, Vic and Ray. Of course Biggs was very inexperienced at the time and his opportunities in Division One racing were restricted to just 2 matches, from which he gleaned 6 points.

He returned to the UK in 1948, having enjoyed an excellent season back in his native land and it was now a different Jack Biggs who lined up for the London outfit. Indeed, Harringay ended the season occupying the runner-up position, ironically behind New Cross, and Jack was singled out by many leading speedway journalists as a rider who had done exceptionally well. From 21 league matches he accrued 102 points for an average of 6.38 and even managed a paid maximum (10+2 points) in an away encounter with Wembley on 27 May.

In 1949 it was something of a surprise when he was transferred to Odsal (Bradford), but as things turned out the West Yorkshire team had acquired a top-class heat-leader and as the season progressed so did the Australian. He went on to record 8 maximums (7 full and 1 paid) on his way to an impressive league average of 8.73 for the then-nicknamed Boomerangs, having netted 326 points from 39 matches. He remained with Odsal in 1950, when he slightly increased his league average to 8.78 and also qualified for his first World Final, scoring 3 points in the Wembley showdown. Moving on to the World Final of twelve months later on 20 September 1951, when 93,000 spectators packed into Wembley Stadium, it will always be remembered as the one that got away as far as Biggs was concerned, and many old-time speedway supporters still talk about it to this day. Jack, who had returned to Harringay in time for the start of the season, had reeled off 4 excellent race wins and needed just a single point to take the crown. However, in his last outing he got into trouble on the first bend and was tailed off. He had a second bite of the cherry though, for a title run-off was necessary against Harringay team-mate Split Waterman and Jack Young, the brilliant Australian from Second Division Edinburgh, all three men having tied on 12-point tallies. Although Biggs duly made the gate, he was chased and passed in sensational fashion by Young, and on the last bend of the race Waterman roared by to deny him second place too. On the domestic front, Jack was a consistent scorer for the Racers and he was to remain with the club until their closure at the end of 1954, his four-year stint there yielding a total of 797 points from 109 league appearances. The enforced change of scenery saw him identified with West Ham in 1955, but his league scoring dipped dramatically and he ended the term with just 65 points to his name.

Then came 1956, when Poole gained promotion to the First Division, with new and experienced top-line riders required by the go-ahead promotional duo of Geoffrey Bravery and Len Matchan. The Pirates were allocated Biggs by the Speedway Control Board and also signed brothers Bert and Cyril Roger from West Ham and Norwich respectively. However, Jack wasn't happy with his posting as he wanted to be with a London track and he said so forceably. To his credit he did stay with the Dorset club – there was no withholding of services until he got his own way, and it turned out to be one of the best things he ever did.

After a poorish time with West Ham, Jack really came into his own at Poole and right from the beginning he proved to be the experienced heat-leader that the Pirates wanted. For a time the side was challenging near the top of the table, although they eventually fell away to finish sixth in the seven-team league. Jack remained ever-present throughout the 24-match league programme and it was little surprise that he ended the campaign on top of the averages with a figure of 8.64, having gleaned a total of 225 points. He had clearly been a success story and to prove he was a fast rider too, on 18 June he also managed to equal the Poole track record of 70.0 seconds, established by Swedish star Olle Nygren almost five years previously in August 1951. Aside from these achievements, the year also saw him claim a reserve spot in the World Final to add to previous appearances in the main meeting in 1950, 1951, 1953 and 1954.

It came as a tremendous shock to the patrons of Poole Speedway when, in 1957, the promoters decided they couldn't continue and one of the sport's most well-known clubs, together with both Wembley and Odsal, closed down. Poole, however, did run 7 meetings on an open licence and Rayleigh even staged a couple of their league matches on the Wimborne Road circuit in the hope of attracting bigger crowds. Jack spent the season with Oxford, along with his protégé, Ray Cresp, and he enjoyed his stay with the Cheetahs, plundering 158 league points to finish as runner-up to Ronnie Genz (171) in the side's scoring. 1957 also saw him again qualify as reserve for the World Final, although as in the previous year he didn't get to ride on the big night.

League racing returned to Poole in 1958, with Vic Gooden bringing his entire Rayleigh outfit down to Dorset, and he was happy to see Jack Biggs allocated to his new Pirates side by the Speedway Control Board. This time around nobody was more pleased to be back at Poole than the Aussie and his zest was demonstrated on the track as he flew to 158 points to head the club's scorechart. Despite his sterling

efforts it was a tough season for Poole and they only just avoided the wooden spoon, finishing ninth in the ten-team National League. Vic Gooden remained in charge for 1959 but this was not a good year for Biggs as he dropped to fourth place in the scorers' list with 83 points in league racing. Ironically, Ray Cresp had joined the Pirates after a season in the colours of Ipswich, and he topped the club's scoring stakes with 143 points. Unfortunately, Jack's problems were of a medical nature as he was suffering from an internal complaint and often turned out when far from fully fit.

The whole Poole set-up changed in 1960, when Charlie Knott Snr took a lease on the stadium and entered the Pirates in the newly-formed Provincial League. Vic Gooden, meanwhile, stayed in the National League by moving his outfit to Ipswich. Things didn't work out for Biggs at Foxhall Heath and after recording only 12 league points for the Witches he saw out the season back at Oxford, with Colin Gooddy moving in the opposite direction as part of the deal. The move did him the power of good and his 100-point tally played a big part in the Cheetahs' final league position of third place. Still with Oxford the following term, Jack was restricted to 80 league points due again to indifferent health which in the end meant a hernia operation. Just 82 points followed for the Cheetahs in 1962, when his form almost deserted him, and when

he subsequently linked with Coventry he really struggled in the league, gleaning points tallies of 29 and 37 in 1963 and 1964 respectively. Amazingly in 1965, the formation of the British League gave him a new lease of life and, having been allocated to Newport, he scorched to the top of their scoring with 280 points for a league average of 9.05. After serving the Welsh side well with another 159 points in 1966, the Rider Control Committee struck and Jack was posted to Cradley Heath. He only stayed with the Heathens long enough to knock up 62 league points before announcing his retirement towards the end of May. The Australian wasn't out of leathers for long though, as he was later identified back in the Metropolis, scoring 18 points from 3 league matches for Hackney. Jack was to stay with the London club for a further two years until he was unluckily sidelined by a broken pelvis in 1970. Having recovered fitness, and still unable to give up the sport he loved, he again returned to active racing in his native country. Sadly, on 8 December 1972 at the age of fifty, he died after sustaining multiple injuries in a crash at Bendigo, a track situated 100 miles from his Melbourne home. To this day, many Poole supporters still remember his outstanding performances wearing the famous Skull and Crossbones breastplate between 1956 and 1959 and recall this most likeable of riders fondly.

Born: 16 October 1966, Farnham, Surrey

Competition	Matches	Points
League	132	1,035
Knock-Out Cup	8	66
Others	23	199
Four-team tournaments	24	137
Pirates total	**187**	**1,437**

David Graham Biles initially had an interest in grass-track racing, and one day, whilst competing in an event at Andover Airfield, he was spotted by the legendary Lew Coffin. Thus, in 1983, David followed Lew to his famous training school at Weymouth, and after some intense tuition the youngster had done sufficiently well to claim a spot in the Wildcats side. Although it was hard going, Biles revealed great determination and, at the end of the season, he had ridden in 16 league matches and accumulated 35 points. The Dorset side enjoyed an excellent run in the Knock-Out Cup and battled past Boston, Glasgow and Newcastle on their way to the final, where they met Exeter. David was a member of the side for both legs of the decider, but in a gripping showdown it was the Falcons who came out on top, by the smallest of margins in the end, winning 96-95 on aggregate.

After showing such promise in his first year, Biles was a Weymouth regular from the off in 1984, and in fact he remained ever-present throughout the 30-match league programme, notching a very impressive tally of 214 points for a healthy 7.13 average. He had developed his own tough riding style and, with all his points earned through sheer hard graft, had become a real crowd-pleaser at Radipole Lane. Future redevelopment at the stadium had been mooted, but it was still a surprise in early 1985 when promoters Mervyn Stewkesbury and Pete Ansell moved the entire Weymouth operation to Poole, and in the process introduced National League racing to Wimborne Road. The move proved a smart one, with the Poole public taking the new standard of racing to their hearts, albeit with the Wildcats moniker replacing the traditional Pirates nickname.

David was, of course, one of the riders who moved with the former Weymouth set-up and he was to play an important role in kick-starting the speedway scene at Poole. His first appearance for his new club was in the opening home meeting of the season, a challenge match versus Milton Keynes on 5 April. Run on a heavy circuit, the Wildcats secured a 45-33 success, with Biles' contribution being 3+1 points from 4 starts. In spite of this somewhat low-key beginning, he worked hard to master his new home strip and really came into his own on 11 June when Poole entertained Rye House in a league encounter. The match resulted in a fine 55-23 win for the home team and in a personal triumph for the Surrey boy he netted his initial paid maximum (10+2 points) in the sport. He followed that up with a paid full-house against Milton Keynes (8+4) at home on 30 July, with the icing on the cake undoubtedly being an unbeaten 10+2 return at Long Eaton on 28 August as the Wildcats romped to a 51-27 victory. With Poole boasting some high-powered scorers in Stan Bear, Kevin Smith and Martin Yeates, the battle for the Championship was a hot one, although in the end the title went the way of Ellesmere Port by just a single point. David had a good first term with Poole, riding in a full quota of 36 league matches to yield an average of 6.52, having accrued 191 points. Poole were again involved in the shake-up at the head of the league in 1986, but in the end they had to settle for the runners-up spot for a second successive year, 6 points adrift of Eastbourne. The Wildcats had a top four equal to any in the league, and with Biles upping his average to 7.88 courtesy of 275 points, he was rightly included in that bracket. He also totalled 48 bonus points, which was by far the most recorded by any Poole rider, and this clearly demonstrated his ability to team-ride when the occasion demanded it.

The Pirates moniker was restored in 1987, but unfortunately it didn't inspire the team to greater things, as they slipped down to eighth place in the final league standings. However, for David it proved a great year, as he and Steve Schofield enjoyed a healthy rivalry at the top of the club's scoring stakes. 'Schoie' ended up in the number one position with a 9.62 average, but Biles wasn't far behind on 9.25, having accumulated 258 points from 29 league fixtures. Perhaps his finest ride occurred on 20 October, when the Wimborne Road raceway played host to a farewell meeting for Poole

legend Martin Yeates, featuring a team match between the Megastars and the Superstars. Riding for the Superstars was World Champion Hans Nielsen and in heat 13, David, who was in the Megastars septet, produced an inspired effort to defeat the 'Main Dane'. True, the conditions were pretty poor due to rain, but there was no disputing his win. Everyone in speedway knew that Nielsen always rode to win, so Biles' triumph was fair and square, with the brilliant Dane being the first to congratulate him on the warm-down lap.

His league average slipped a tad to 8.51 in 1988, but with a total of 311 points from 30 matches it could still be regarded as a more-than-satisfactory campaign. He again finished second to Steve Schofield in the Poole statistics and his riding was catching the eye of a number of promoters from the top flight, who were ever on the lookout for up-and-coming riders. However, they, and as it transpired the Poole management, were to be disappointed, since the call of the family business came. They were farmers at Grateley, near Andover, and David had grown up helping his father. So at the end of 1988, farming's gain was speedway's loss, as he gave up the bikes for a full-time job on the land. Had he chosen to remain in the sport, there is little doubt he would have made it to the higher echelons. As a thrill-maker he had few peers and as a result many terrace folk often referred to him as Dave 'Boy' Biles, but perhaps 'Boy oh Boy' Biles would have been even more appropriate!

Born: 3 May 1923, Chigwell, Essex

Competition	Matches	Points
League	36	270
National Trophy	4	60
Others	2	21
Four-team tournaments	1	3
Pirates total	**43**	**354**

Joseph Leonard Bowkis first became interested in speedway whilst serving in the Army. His first rides on the track took place in Hamburg, Germany, where it was a case of using any machine he could find. Being only 5ft 2in in stature, he was known as 'Little Joe', and he quickly became proficient at the discipline. After serving for five years in the Royal Corps of Signals, with whom besides Germany he also saw service in Belgium, France, Denmark and Holland, he decided to take up the sport seriously. Despite having no bike of his own in the first instance, Joe borrowed one and duly set off to Rye House for bags and bags of practice under the watchful eye of Dicky Case. This was in 1947 and the sport was still booming, with promoters very much on the lookout for talent. The lad from Chigwell caught the eye of Harringay boss Fred Whitehead, who offered him a contract with his First Division outfit.

Bowkis made his league debut for the Racers in a home encounter against Odsal (Bradford) on 16 May and, although he failed to trouble the scorers, he impressed sufficiently to retain his place in the side. He went on to make a total of 11 league appearances, from which he accrued 8 points for an average of 1.48. While continuing to progress, he furthered his experience at Rye House, winning both the Lish Trophy and the Rye House Championship. It was felt that he would benefit from gaining experience at a lower level and the opportunity arose when Poole joined the Third Division in 1948. The Dorset club had established links with Harringay and the Londoners had already aided the Pirates' team-building by loaning them promising juniors Fred Pawson and Sid Clark. So it transpired that Bowkis also travelled down to Poole for the official practice and

was promptly signed on. However, his signing wasn't in time for him to race for the Pirates in their very first match at Tamworth on 14 April, a league fixture, and there is no doubt Poole could have done with his services since they went down to a crushing 63-21 defeat.

It was on 26 April that Poole opened its doors to the sport for the first time and Joe made his debut as a Pirate, sporting the number five race-jacket in a National Trophy tie against Great Yarmouth. No-one in the 6,000 audience was prepared for the dramatic events of the first-ever race when visiting rider Reg Craven fell on the first bend and was inadvertently run into by Poole's Charlie Hayden, who was simply unable to avoid him. Sadly, the visiting rider suffered severe head injuries in the impact and subsequently succumbed to them eight days later on 4 May. Despite the accident, the meeting carried on and the race formula for the competition meant that Bowkis took his opening ride in heat 7, which he won in fine style. His next programmed race was in the very next heat, and amazingly he raced to victory in that one too. His form was nothing short of sensational and he again took the honours when winning his third outing in heat 11. Joe's fourth outing occurred in heat 13 and

there was no stopping him as he won with ease, before incredibly storming to victory in his fifth ride. Unsurprisingly, he was nominated for the final race of the match, heat 18, but his great run came to an end when he failed to finish. Still, a 15-point tally on his debut represented a great start and he ended the night in superb fashion when he took the chequered flag in the Highest Points Scorers' race which closed the meeting. The following evening Poole raced in the second leg of the tie at Caister Road and Bowkis was again in sparkling form, racing to another 15 points and only missing out on a maximum due to machine trouble in heat 15.

Joe had undoubtedly made an excellent start to his career as a Pirate and when Charlie Hayden resigned the team captaincy he was elected to take his place, and became an excellent skipper too. He went on to be one of the very best riders in Division Three, leading his charges from the front and generally scoring well on all the circuits. His excellent form was recognised by the Control Board, who nominated him to meet Gil Blake of Stoke for the Third Division Match Race Championship. This took place at the Potteries venue on 23 September, but unfortunately, on a very wet track, Bowkis crashed and suffered injury. As a result he was out of action for a spell and the Stoke management generously allowed one of their riders, Dick Howard, to join Poole as a replacement. Joe returned to action late in October and his final analysis for the year revealed a healthy total of 270 points from 36 league matches as he made ready for a second term in the famous Skull and Crossbones breast-plate. However, he had also made three appearances for Harringay during the year and, having noted his excellent progress in the lower league, the Racers hierarchy recalled him to race full-time for them in the cut-and-thrust of the First Division in 1949. Regrettably for Joe, his season with Harringay was not a success. He really struggled at times and was unable to hold down a team place on a regular basis. Scoring proved hard and he ended the campaign with a tally of just 33 points to his name from 22 league matches.

Although he rode in a single league match for the Racers at the start of the following season, after such a difficult time in 1949, it came as little surprise when the London outfit said they would listen to offers for him. Pirates chief Cliff Brewer was keen to bring the popular Bowkis back to Wimborne Road, but, to his astonishment, the rider was transferred to Leicester. Mr Brewer was sure he had got his man and was actually saving the news as a surprise for the Poole patrons. However, writing in the programme when Leicester visited with Joe in their line-up, the Pirates boss admitted it was he who had had the surprise when he learned the rider had gone to the Hunters. 'I just don't know how these things are done,' was the comment from an obviously disappointed Mr Brewer. With Joe netting 155 league points, he helped Leicester to third position in the final table of 1950, one place behind Poole. Champions Oxford gained promotion and with the Pirates opting for another year in the Third Division, it was the Hunters who accompanied the Cheetahs into Division Two racing along with both Liverpool and newcomers Motherwell. Bowkis was to remain on board with the Hunters, gleaning totals of 125 and 216 points from league racing in 1951 and 1952 respectively. Unfortunately, he suffered from an internal complaint which required surgery and, in 1953, he retired from speedway after scoring only 7 points for the Midlanders, although he was reputed to be driving stock cars.

Going back to 1952, when Poole took the Second Division title (having been promoted as Champions of Division Three the year before), the season at Wimborne Road ended on 20 October with a challenge match against a select side entitled 'Stars of Division Two'. Joe rode for the composite side and was given a great reception by the fans who had not forgotten his sterling efforts of 1948, when he had earned the nickname of 'Look Back Bowkis' due to his habit of taking a quick peek to see just where all the other riders were lying in the heat of the battle. Such an act was actually against the rules at the time, but he was pretty quick in taking a look and wasn't often caught by the steward in charge! With 4 points to his name, the returnee was on the winning side in that final meeting of 1952, as the Stars of Division Two beat a powerful Pirates side by 44 points to 40 – the only time defeat was suffered down Poole way all season!

Craig Boyce

Born: 2 August 1967, Sydney, New South Wales, Australia.

Competition	Matches	Points
League	293	3,098
Knock-Out Cup	42	480
Others	85	833
Four-team tournaments	41	300
Pirates total	**461**	**4,711**

Craig Boyce first got into speedway in 1985 and such was his progress that just three years later he came to the UK to link with National League competitors Poole, having been recommended by knowledgeable team boss Neil Street. Any young Australian who caught the eye of the wily veteran was immediately referred to the Pirates' management and, for their part, Mervyn Stewkesbury and Pete Ansell were often quick to respond. The signing of 'Boycie' was to be a shrewd one as he was to give the club wonderful service over a number of years, and to this day he proudly holds the record as Poole's all-time highest points plunderer. Looking back, it is strange to relate that he failed to score in his first match for the Dorset side, but he certainly made up for it afterwards. That rather inauspicious debut occurred on 1 April 1988, when he took three point-less outings against Exeter in an Easter Trophy fixture at Wimborne Road. Despite his 'duck', the fans and management were impressed with his all-out efforts, which left no one in any doubt that the points would come. Indeed, just three days after his failure to score against Exeter, he journeyed to the Falcons'

home for the return match, where the sweeping bends of the County Ground circuit really suited him. This, together with some sound advice from Neil Street, who himself had started his British racing career with Exeter way back in 1952, saw Craig score 9 points from 5 outings and he was on his way.

As the weeks went by he rose through the ranks from the reserve berth to a heat-leader position and by the end of the season he had recorded 236 points from 27 matches for a league average of 7.88. The highlight of his initial term on these shores was undoubtedly a first paid maximum (12+3 points) and this happened on 16 August, when the Pirates walloped Middlesbrough 65-31 in a National League encounter at Wimborne Road.

To say he developed rapidly in 1989 would be an understatement, as Boyce registered a total of 342 points to head Poole's league averages with a superb 9.41 figure, just ahead of another Australian find, Leigh Adams (9.19). In what was a glorious year, the Pirates' duos efforts, combined with the form of Alun Rossiter, Alastair Stevens and Gary Allan in particular, helped them to claim the League Championship ahead of Wimbledon.

Craig went on to establish himself as the very top man in the National League in 1990, and few were his equal around any circuit. In what was a wonderful campaign, he scorched to a total of 456 points from 32 meetings for an outstanding 10.54 average, as the Pirates repeated their league title success by an amazing 12 clear points. Not only that but they also won the Knock-Out Cup, and on their way to that triumph, Boyce remarkably scorched to a seven-ride paid maximum (19+2 points) against Middlesbrough in the home leg of the final on 18 September. Just after the season had closed, Craig agreed to a move into the British League and joined Oxford for the furtherance of his career. Rather ironically, the two different leagues were soon to amalgamate, with Poole being one of four teams who moved into the newly-formed First Division to race alongside Oxford in 1991.

Prior to the beginning of the new season he became Australian Champion when he recorded a 15-point maximum at Arunga Park, Northern Territory, on 27 January. Following that success, Boycie made a truly amazing debut meeting for the Cheetahs, scorching to a 17-point tally from 6 rides at King's Lynn in a Gold Cup match on 23 March. Unluckily, after such a great start, his season was marred by a back injury sustained in a nasty track crash in heat 12 of the Ancit Commonwealth Final, also at King's Lynn, on 2 June. He was to miss a huge chunk of the season and only actually rode in 10 league matches for the Cheetahs.

Putting a somewhat dispiriting year behind him, he returned to Poole in 1992, ending the campaign with an impressive top-flight average of 8.77 from 23 league matches. He stayed with the Pirates for another two years, and although his league average dipped to 7.48 in 1993, a resurgence saw him post an excellent 9.14 figure in 1994. That season also saw him reach what was to be the last traditional-style World Final at Vojens, Denmark, and in a tremendous showing he scored 12 points to finish level with Tony Rickardsson and Hans Nielsen at the top of the tree, thus forcing a run-off for the title. There was no fairy-tale ending though, as Rickardsson duly took victory from Nielsen, but third place was still a personal triumph for Craig.

There was a shock for the Poole fans prior to the 1995 season, when Boycie was loaned out to Swindon and installed as captain of the Robins in the 21-team Premier League. He was to have a truly fabulous year for the Wiltshire side, grabbing double-figure scores in all but 2 league meetings to end up with an average of 10.05, having gleaned a mammoth 388 points. On the world stage, he appeared in the inaugural Grand Prix series, and aside from attaining a tally of 60 points for eleventh place

overall, he is probably best remembered for an incident that occurred in the British round at the London Stadium (formerly Hackney) on 30 September. The sparks really flew in the 'C' final when, after Craig had driven under Tomasz Gollob, the Pole came back and left him sprawling after a robust challenge. Clearly angered by the incident, Boyce subsequently approached Gollob and a right-hand punch sent the Polish flyer crashing to the ground. All this was caught by the cameras of Sky television and to this day it remains much talked about in the world of speedway.

Back in his homeland, Craig landed a second Australian title when scoring a full 15-pointer at the Newcastle Showground, New South Wales, on 17 February 1996. After his successful stint with Swindon, Craig returned once more to Poole and with 403 points, he topped the team's league averages on a high 9.30 figure. Meanwhile, in the Grand Prix, he managed a series total of 30 points, his best performance being a third-place finish in the 'B' final in Italy. Seeing out the year in fine style, he then completed a hat-trick of Australian titles, with a five-ride full-house at the Brisbane Exhibition, Queensland, on 28 December.

Boyce again scored freely for the Pirates in 1997, when he held on to his mantle as the club's number one rider, with 381 points yielding a league average of 9.11. Although he was a little less productive in 1998, he still netted a further 288 points in the cause of the Skull and Crossbones, which calculated to a league average of 7.13. Believe it or not that was his lowest figure for the Pirates in the nine full seasons he had represented the club. Having missed out on the 1997 Grand Prix series, Craig made his last assault on the sport's premier event in 1998, but he enjoyed little success, ending up with just 18 points from six rounds.

So to 1999, and it was at this point in his career that the Aussie was to begin moving about to earn his living in speedway. He spent the year with Oxford before linking with King's Lynn in 2000. Then, in 2001, he joined Ipswich and was more than happy to again don the blue and white of Poole for a couple of guest outings. Remaining with Ipswich in

2002, Boyce proved he could still 'mix it' amongst the cream of the Elite League, as he raced to 262 points for a solid 7.48 average in what was his fifteenth year of racing in the UK. It must have been a huge disappointment when he learned he wasn't in the immediate Ipswich team plans for 2003, but in what was a deserved Testimonial season he was welcomed back at Poole as skipper of their British

League Cup side. With the competition running on different lines to the usual domestic fare, he was also permitted to ride for Oxford in the Elite League. However, following changes to the Oxford line-up, the man from Down Under was eventually recalled by Ipswich, having ridden in just 9 matches for the Silver Machine outfit. Although his best form eluded him for the Witches, all the while he was riding well in the British League Cup, accumulating 121 points from 13 matches and doing his bit to help Poole win the trophy, thanks to an aggregate final victory over Eastbourne. Prior to that, on 27 August, a crowd of some 5,000 packed the Wimborne Road rafters to pay tribute at his big Testimonial meeting, with Jason Crump coming out on top in an all-star line-up, ahead of Leigh Adams, Billy Hamill and Tony Rickardsson. Ultimately, the Pirates had a marvellous season of success, for aside from their British League Cup triumph, they also won the Elite League Championship and the Knock-Out Cup. A guest appearance in the league, plus a couple of outings in challenge matches and one in a four-team tournament took Craig's total of club appearances to 461, and helped swell his points record to a mammoth 4,711 – a truly fabulous achievement.

Born: 11 February 1919, Christchurch, Dorset

Competition	Matches	Points
League	75	570
National Trophy	8	79
Others	7	64
Three and four-team tournaments	2	4
Pirates total	**92**	**717**

Alan Chambers initially began racing on the grass tracks in the Southern and Western Centres. He became interested in speedway during 1946 and joined the winter training school successfully run at Bristol's Knowle Stadium by former West Ham skipper Tiger Stevenson. Such was Alan's progress that Exeter, who were busy team-building for entry to the newly-formed Third Division in 1947, quickly signed him on. For good measure, the Falcons also signed three other Bournemouth-based riders in Charlie Hayden, Sid Hazzard and Tom Crutcher. The son of the latter, Brian, was to burst on to the speedway scene in outstanding style during 1951 when only sixteen years of age.

On 14 April 1947, Exeter staged an individual meeting billed as the 'Battle for Team Places', in which Chambers did particularly well to glean a 10-point tally. Eight days later, the County Ground circuit played host to a Possibles versus Probables match, which the former won 44-37. Plundering 11 points, Alan was top scorer for the losing Probables side and a place in the Exeter team was his. Four challenge matches later, the Falcons opened their league campaign at home to Hanley (Stoke) on 12 May, when they trounced the Potteries outfit 62-20. Alan helped himself to 10 points in the scoring spree, and in the return fixture on 15 May he topped the scorechart with 9 points in a 49-33 defeat. After such a good start in their colours, Alan became a regular in the Falcons line-up and he went on to record a total of 156 league points as the side occupied fourth position out of eight in the final table.

With Poole set to open for Division Three racing in 1948, Chambers was transferred to his local side for a reported fee of £90, while fellow Bournemouth-based speedsters Sid Hazzard, Charlie Hayden and Tom Crutcher also linked with the Pirates. Tragically, Crutcher (who was also set to be part of the promotional team) was to lose his life in a road traffic accident during the winter months, but the other three riders were in the Poole team for the opening meeting, a league match at Tamworth on 14 April. It turned out to be a baptism of fire for the Pirates as they went down to a 63-21 mauling, with Alan's contribution being just 3 points. Poole duly opened their doors for the first time to the cinder sport on 26 April, when Great Yarmouth provided the opposition in a National Trophy tie. Chambers was in splendid form in front of his new fans, scoring 15+2 points from 6 outings, with his only defeat suffered at the hands of Paddy Hammond in heat 12. Riding stylishly, he proved a steady scorer for the Pirates and remained ever-present throughout the 44-match league campaign, during which he gleaned a total of 318 points and played an important part in the establishing of Poole Speedway.

Before the end of the season, Alan accompanied his team-mates on a short tour of Sweden, where they raced in 3 matches. The first at Linkoping saw the home side win 45-27, but Chambers did well for the Pirates, heading the scoring with a dozen points. The next encounter against Eskilstuna saw Alan claim 9 points in a 30-30 draw, although the meeting was variously described as having more of an individual nature than a team match. The third and final fixture took the Pirates to Stockholm, where they gained a hard-fought 36-33 success, thanks largely to Chambers' total of 12 points from 5 outings.

During the 1948/49 close season, Alan was part of a company of riders, mainly from the Third Division, who travelled to South Africa for a series of unofficial Test matches. Billed as South Africa v. England, the sides met on 5 occasions, with 3 of the meetings staged at Johannesburg and the other 2 held in Benoni. England surged to a 4-1 victory in the series and Chambers clearly showed an appetite for the racing by heading his country's scoring with 47 points from the 5-match stint. However, he was to enjoy more than just the racing side of things in South Africa, for he fell in love with the country and was to make his home there in 1949.

Before that, Alan was back in a Skull and Crossbones race-jacket and very quickly ran into high-scoring form with 12+1 points, as the Pirates demolished newly-formed Halifax 70-38 in a National Trophy tie at Wimborne Road on 11 April. The return match against the Dukes took place in West Yorkshire on 20 April and Poole rode in outstanding fashion to win 59-48 for a crushing aggregate success. Chambers clearly enjoyed himself on the steeply-banked Shay circuit and with a tally of 9 points gave excellent support to his team-mates Cyril Quick (14) and Fred Pawson (13+2).

Swindon Speedway opened-up at Blunsdon for the very first time on 23 July and the following week Poole visited the Abbey Stadium for a challenge match. The Pirates ran riot to win 58-25, and Alan not only established a new track record of 81.4 seconds in the opening heat, but went on to register a sparkling paid maximum (10+2). The points kept on coming and there was an extra-special evening for him on 22 August when Plymouth visited Wimborne Road for a league match. The first race saw Chambers simply rocket around the 420-yard track to equal Billy Bales' record time of 76.4 seconds for the circuit. He went on to record 9+1 points in a 49-35 victory, but for Poole supporters, and indeed for Alan himself, it was a sad occasion as he had booked a passage on board the ship *Warwick Castle* to return to South Africa with his family. He had decided to make a permanent home there and had tried to book a later voyage for the end of the season, but with this unfortunately not being possible it was a fond farewell to the Poole public. At the time of his departure he had ridden in 31 league matches for the Pirates, carding 252 points in the process, and had long since been looked upon as an excellent team man. At the end of the season an England team again toured South Africa to appear in a Test series and lining up for the 'Springboks', having changed nationality, was one Alan Chambers, who again rode in all 5 matches, netting 38 points. Only two South African riders scored better than Alan and both were to do well in British speedway: they were Fred Wills, with Liverpool and later Stoke, and Henry Long, who not only rose to the rank of a heat-leader with Belle Vue but also appeared in the 1952 World Final, scoring 7 points. Alan never again rode for Poole or any other side in the UK, and although it was reported that he was prepared to come over in 1950, regrettably this never materialised.

Born: 11 July 1964, Whitstable, Kent

Competition	Matches	Points
League	82	813
Knock-Out Cup	19	173
Others	51	568
Three and four-team tournaments	9	80
Pirates total	**161**	**1,634**

Marvyn Cox's initial link with a career in speedway came about due to the interest shown by Jim Smith, the father of former Rye House and Poole rider Kevin. Having developed into a useful competitor on the junior grass-track scene, Marvyn took his first rides on the shale at Rye House and immediately showed great promise. The date of 2 April 1981 proved a red-letter day: promoter Len Silver handed him a debut for the Rockets in a challenge match at Oxford, and he grabbed the opportunity to score 2+1 points from a couple of starts. He went on to hold down a regular place in the side, finishing the season with 129 points from 34 National League matches for an impressive 4.81 average. Two particular highlights from his first campaign were a 12-point maximum at home to Workington on 27 September and a paid full-house (8+4) when Peterborough visited the Hoddesdon raceway on 4 October. Such was his rate of progress in 1982 that he filled the role of a heat-leader with Rye House and even enjoyed an outing for promoter Len Silver's other track, Hackney, in the higher echelons of the British League. Given the fact it was only his second year in the sport his record was nothing short of phenomenal for the Rockets, as he netted 245 points to post a league average of 8.92.

'Cocker', as he was nicknamed, continued to raise his game the following year when recording a massive 457 league points to average 9.88 for Rye House, while also furthering his top-flight experience with several more outings for Hackney. A full-time move into the higher sphere of domestic racing beckoned in 1984, but it didn't turn out to be with the Hawks. Instead, it was with Oxford, who had

taken over the British League licence of the London track from Len Silver. The former Hackney boss duly took over as team manager of the Cheetahs, with Hans Nielsen and Simon Wigg spearheading the new-look side. Taking into account Silver's knowledge of the rider, he naturally wanted Cox at Oxford too, and at the request of club number one Hans Nielsen, the lad from Whitstable became his riding partner at number two. There is no doubting the fact that Marvyn grew in both confidence and track craft alongside the 'Main Dane', with the superb team-riding of the duo reaching legendary status amongst the Cheetahs' fans. In a highly satisfactory year, Cocker amassed 162 points for a 6.19 league average. Not only that, he also defeated Simon Cross in a run-off to win the British Under-21 Championship at Canterbury, prior to being crowned World Under-21 Champion ahead of Neil Evitts in the final at King's Lynn.

Over the next two seasons Oxford carried all before them to take consecutive league titles, and while Marvyn's league average only increased marginally to 6.44 in 1985, it shot right up to 8.79 in 1986. Despite persistent rumours that he wanted to leave Oxford, Cox was to stay with the Cowley-based club for the next three seasons, riding well and filling whatever role his bosses wanted as they played the 'numbers game' due to the maximum-points ceiling. During this period Marvyn garnered another 599 points from 87 domestic matches, taking his overall league tally to 1,031 points over a six-year spell with the Cheetahs.

A change of scenery saw Cocker join Bradford for 1990 and he became the club's leading rider, scoring 313 points from 30 league matches for an 8.88 average. The Odsal circuit was completely different to what he had been used to at Oxford, but he rose to the challenge and was suitably dubbed 'Marvellous Marvyn Cox' by the Dukes' supporters. After such a successful year he was expected to stay with the West Yorkshire outfit, but it was Poole who, having stepped up to join the new First Division, snapped up his services and made him skipper in 1991. The Pirates didn't boast a particularly strong side and finished the campaign occupying tenth spot out of the thirteen competing teams. Marvyn was quite superb, however, and in doing a fine job of leading the attack he totalled 258 league points to yield an average of 8.63. Some of his showings were simply breathtaking, the most prominent being a 15-point maximum at Swindon on 20 July, and similar scores against both Reading and Coventry when they visited Dorset on 13 August and 3 September respectively. On top of that he added his name to the illustrious list of Blue Riband victors, scoring 12 points to take the trophy ahead of Gary Havelock.

After such an excellent first season representing the Skull and Crossbones, Cox really came into his own in 1992. The Wimborne Road bosses strengthened the team, and with better back-up than he'd received the year before, Marvyn enjoyed a wonderful campaign. In a season of top-class performances he really sparkled at King's Lynn on 6 June when, although the Pirates lost 49-41, he went through the card unbeaten for a 6-ride full-

house. He repeated this feat at Eastbourne on 12 July, helping Poole on that occasion to achieve a 45-45 draw. It was a much better term for the side in their quest for league honours, since they jumped up to third spot, and Cocker could look back with much satisfaction, having notched 285 points for a league average of 9.41. Little did anyone know at the end of the season, but it was to be over four years before he again donned a Pirates race-jacket.

With a riders' pay policy introduced, Marvyn was unable to agree terms for 1993 and duly based himself in Germany, where he took out a German racing licence. He was seemingly lost to the sport in this country, but he continued to ply his trade on the Continent, even winning the German Championship on two occasions (1993 and 1995). Cox made a brief return to these shores in 1995, when he helped out a Reading side which had lost the services of David Norris through injury. Despite heavy commitments, he did a splendid job to average 9.44 from 7 league matches and there was regret on both sides when he left due to a combination of poor crowds, the cost of fares and a lack of sponsorship.

Marvyn did make a full-time comeback to these shores in 1996, however, when he rejoined Oxford in the nineteen-team Premier League. A thirteenth place finish didn't represent the best of seasons for the Cheetahs, but the returnee did his utmost for the side, averaging 8.22 after riding in 32 league matches and recording 333 points.

1997 was the inaugural year of the Elite League and Cox was back with Poole after what had seemed like an eternity to some of the Dorset faithful. It wasn't a good year for the Pirates though, as they ended the campaign as wooden-spoonists in the ten-team league. After struggling with machinery problems, Marvyn was 'rested' in late August as the management searched for a winning combination, but he was invited to return in mid-September after Armando Castagna had asked to be released. Despite everything, Marvyn still scored 250 league points, which was sufficient to make him runner-up to Craig Boyce in the club's scoring stakes. A couple of meetings really stood out along the way, these being a full 18-point haul at King's Lynn on 21 June and a paid maximum (14+1) in a home match against Coventry on 24 September.

Regrettably, 1998 was to be his last year in the saddle, since he suffered a badly broken thigh after crashing in heat 6 of a league match against King's Lynn at Wimborne Road on 27 May. At one time the injury was life-threatening, but thankfully he slowly pulled through. Keeping in contact with the sport, Marvyn later helped to train youngsters on specially built mini-bikes, whilst also being chief helpmate to Australian international Todd Wiltshire. One of the sport's nice guys, he still pays regular visits to Poole, where he is always happy to help out riding pals both old and new.

Aside from numerous international outings for England, on the individual front Marvyn appeared in two World Finals, netting 3 points at Katowice, Poland in 1986 and 9 points at Vojens, Denmark in 1994. He then went on to be a regular in the Grand Prix series during its first two seasons of operation, scoring totals of 54 points in 1995 and 15 points in 1996. Revealing great versatility he was also a six-times finalist in the World Long-track Championship (1989-1992, 1994 and 1995), his best effort being a fourth-place finish in 1995.

Born: 27 June 1946, Palmerston North,
New Zealand

Competition	Matches	Points
League	143	582
Knock-Out Cup	9	46
Others	27	109
Pirates total	**179**	**737**

Whilst at school, Bruce Brian Hoani Cribb proved himself to be an all-round sportsman, playing cricket and rugby with distinction as well as also enjoying both swimming and athletics. He later trained as a motor mechanic before taking his first speedway skids at his local track in 1963. It soon became apparent that Bruce had that 'something special' and when fellow New Zealander Bill Andrew arrived to ride for Poole in the inaugural year of the British League in 1965, he recommended the young 'Cribby' to the forward-looking Pirates' management. The season was well underway when they decided to cable Bruce and in next to no time he had journeyed over to make his debut in a home league match against Edinburgh on 4 August, when, unsurprisingly, he didn't score from his two rides. What remained of the season was to be a sharp learning curve, but one meeting that did show his distinct promise occurred on 18 August, when Poole met Glasgow in a league encounter at Wimborne Road. His first outing was in heat 4, and there was great excitement amongst a packed audience as he produced a terrific ride to join team-mate Ross Gilbertson on a 5-1. (The Pirates duo in fact finished ahead of Scot Jim McMillan and Bernie Lagrosse, another young Kiwi who later changed his name to Roy Williams and went

on to give good service to Berwick in the Second Division of the British League.) Then, in heat 8, Cribb picked up a point (plus a bonus) when he followed partner Pete Smith across the line behind Glasgow ace Charlie Monk. He failed to score from two further starts, but with a tally of 3+2 points he had made a great impression. By the season's end, Bruce had made 10 league appearances and netted a total 15 points for an average of 3.30.

Remaining with the Pirates in 1966, remarkably he was one of four Kiwis in the side, the others being Bill Andrew and new recruits Colin McKee and Wayne Briggs. There were, however, eight riders in contention for seven places and whilst Cribb definitely made progress as the season progressed, he couldn't command a regular spot in the side. He still made 26 league appearances though, and in recording 64 points he raised his average to 4.15.

Bruce duly became the only New Zealander at Poole in 1967, since Bill Andrew stayed at home while both Wayne Briggs and Colin McKee moved on to Exeter and Hackney respectively. He managed to hold his place in the side on merit too, scoring 111 points from 35 matches for an improved 5.08 league average. The Kiwi enjoyed another year of slow but sure progress in 1968, as he became an excellent 'back-up' rider. With Gote Nordin departing to pursue business matters after just one league match, the Pirates were up against it virtually from the start. Indeed, they fought all year to avoid the wooden spoon and eventually finished seventeeth in the nineteen-team league. Given the circumstances, Cribb was worthy of high praise for posting a 5.50 average, having garnered 127 points from 30 league matches.

If 1968 was disappointing for Poole, then 1969 was the complete opposite. The Dorseteers raced to the British League Championship, taking the title by a 6-point margin from Belle Vue. A red-letter day for the New Zealander came on 30 April, when Hackney provided the opposition for a league match at Wimborne Road. Showing tremendous track craft, he raced through the card to register a first full maximum (12 points), as Poole claimed a 57-21 victory. Proving that was no fluke, another evening to remember happened at Wolverhampton on 8 August, when the Pirates took the unfortunate Wolves to the cleaners in great style, winning 49-29, with the Kiwi being paid for the 'lot' (9+3 points). Bruce appeared in each and every one of the 36 league meetings, and played a big part in the club's glory, tallying 227 points for an average of 7.24. Regrettably, the Pirates success meant their side was broken up in 1970, and this meant a change of scenery for the man from Palmerston North, who subsequently linked with Exeter. Despite this, he was to make several guest appearances for Poole in the ensuing years, although he never rode for the club on a full-time basis again.

Cribb showed great form around Exeter's huge County Ground bowl, and was to finish his first year as a Falcon boasting a league average of 9.31. He didn't manage to scale the dizzy heights of a nine-point average in a further two seasons with the Devon outfit and, in 1973, he was on the move again, linking with Cradley Heath. His best campaign with the Heathens occurred in 1976, when he remained ever-present to achieve a league average of 7.77, having accumulated 288 points.

Bruce remained a regular with Cradley Heath until 1978, when a surprise mid-term change saw him transferred to Bristol. When the season came to a close, Bruce had 86 points and an average of 5.32 to his name from 20 league matches in the Bulldogs colours, and the enthusiastic West Country supporters looked forward to again seeing him in action at 'tapes-up' the following year. However, the club was beset with problems, and on 18 December came the news that the best-supported track in Britain was no more. That meant another move for the New Zealander, and, after joining Wolverhampton for 1979, he raced in 32 league matches for 167 points and a 5.94 average. A real highlight that year saw the legendary Ivan Mauger lead New Zealand to glory in the World Team Cup Final at London's White City Stadium on 16 September, and Bruce played his part in their success, notching a 5-point tally.

Again, the Kiwi raced for Wolverhampton in 1980, when he also made some late-season appearances for Oxford in the National League. With the Wolves subsequently dropping into the National League themselves in 1981, an upsurge in form saw 'Cribby' net 345½ points for a high 9.96 average whilst also 'doubling-up' on several occasions with Birmingham. He then linked with Berwick at their new Berrington Lough home in 1982 and was to remain with the Borders outfit for four years until the end of 1985, during which time he continued to make odd British League outings with Birmingham (1982-1983) and Reading (1984). Bruce certainly enjoyed his spell with the Bandits, riding in a total of 135 league matches and scoring 1,294 points in the process, with his best season being 1984, when he posted a 9.13 average.

Aside from the occasional match in the British League, he was to see out his racing days with a three-year stint back at Exeter (1986-1988), during which he raced in 45 league matches for 370 points, with the last couple of seasons being particularly hampered by injury. During his elongated service to the sport, Bruce not only performed at international level for his native New Zealand, but also Great Britain, the Rest of the World and Australasia, as well as Scotland at National League level! He was also an accomplished ice racer, and there was no more thrilling sight than the Kiwi mounted on his spike-tyred machine, shattering track records in demonstration rides at conventional shale circuits. He was certainly a robust character – this was endorsed by his former Exeter team-mate of 1971 and 1972, Bob Kilby, who once said of him: 'Cribby was one of the toughest riders I ever met and he was as strong as an ox too. When it came to riding on tracks that were either wet, rough, full of holes or generally poor, I never saw anyone handle the conditions better than he.'

Born: 23 August 1934, Parkstone, nr Poole, Dorset

Competition	Matches	Points
League	88	689
National Trophy	12	133
Others	22	170
Four-team tournaments	1	6
Pirates total	**123**	**998**

Brian Crutcher, like many other cinder-shifters, began his racing interests in the world of cycle speedway. A local boy, he started his speedway career in earnest at the old Ringwood track on Boxing Day 1950 when just sixteen years of age, and it was immediately clear that he had that extra 'something' which makes good riders great.

Brian burst upon the scene at Poole in spectacular fashion on Tuesday 24 April 1951, when the Pirates faced Exeter in a Festival of Britain Trophy encounter. For this particular competition each team had ten members and Crutcher was included in the Poole side at number ten. His first outing occurred in heat 8, when he and team-mate Allan Kidd met the Falcons duo of Jack Bedkober and Mick Hard – the latter, incidentally, programmed as Maurice Hard in error. Amazingly, the young Pirate raced to the front and went on to win in the impressive time of 75.2 seconds. Throughout the race his partner, Kidd, did a good job covering the teenager but, showing

an ability well beyond his years, Brian proved an excellent winner. His second ride was in heat 12, when he once more partnered Kidd against Hard, with Paul Best being the other Exeter representative. The result was not only a further victory for Crutcher, but also another 5-1 to Poole. An audible murmur went up from the crowd as it was obvious they were watching a star in the making. In heat 19, the penultimate race, he was called upon to replace Jack Cunningham, being partnered on that occasion by Charlie Hayden. Meanwhile, the opposition was supplied by Don Hardy, the Falcons' top man on the night, and Ted Moore. The home supporters held their breath as the young Brian took the lead, closely followed by Hayden, and try as he might there was nothing Hardy could do. So another 5-1 was registered and Poole went on to win the match 70-50, with their young debutant riding unbeaten for a 9-point tally. It was an outstanding performance and from that meeting on he became a regular team member, initially in a reserve berth, although it was clear he wouldn't stay in that position for too long.

When the Pirates visited Ipswich for a challenge match on 14 June, they recorded a fine 50-34 success and Crutcher was the star of the show. He netted 11 points and the Witches' supporters took him to their hearts, so much so that he had to be rescued from dozens of autograph hunters at the end of the evening! His natural ability was again in evidence in a memorable league match at Swindon on 7 July when Poole produced a dazzling display to win 53-31. Brian was second reserve alongside new signing Bill Holden, who had joined via

Southampton. Although a couple of team members were having a quiet time, the reserve duo were unbeaten by an opponent, amassing a paid total of 21 points between them. Crutcher had collected two wins before being brought into the last heat in place of the off-form Dick Howard. He was partnered by his skipper Ken Middleditch, with the Robins represented by two most able riders in Hugh Geddes and Alex Gray. For a couple of laps it was 'Middlo' in the lead ahead of Geddes, while Brian held third spot, trying all the time inside and outside. In the end the Swindon man didn't know from which direction he was coming and as soon as he left a gap Crutcher was through in the twinkling of an eye to join his captain for a maximum advantage.

Wednesday 25 July turned out to be another enjoyable night for fans of the Pirates when their heroes defeated Aldershot 59½-24½ in a league match. There was joy on the terraces following heat 7 when it was announced that Bill Holden had equalled the track record of 72.8 seconds. However, there was even more delight when Crutcher established a new best of 72.6 seconds in heat 13. Brian had acquired two nicknames in a short space of time – to many he was known as the 'Nipper', while others referred to him as the 'Mouse'. As the happy patrons wended their way home after the match against the Shots there was a real buzz, with one phrase repeatedly heard: 'The Mouse has beaten the track record.'

His super form was recognised internationally when he was capped at England 'C' level against both Sweden and the USA. He garnered 7 points against the Swedes at Poole and 2 points versus the USA, also at Wimborne Road, but failed to score in a second match against the Americans at Swindon. Unfortunately, Crutcher's track record didn't last too long because in the aforementioned Test match against Sweden at the Dorset raceway on 13 August, Olle Nygren blitzed around the track in 70 seconds dead.

On 17 September, the Pirates raced at home against Plymouth in a Division Three fixture and it was to prove another memorable day for Brian, since he recorded his first 12-point full-house in a 51-33 victory. He was programmed as second reserve, but took two of Charlie

Hayden's rides and all his wins were posted in fast times. At the end of his first term in the sport he had accrued 209 points from a full quota of 36 league matches for an incredible 9.41 average.

There can be no doubt that 1951 was a season to remember for the youngster. He had claimed a regular place in the Poole side, one that took the Third Division title by 4 points from Exeter; he had scored his first full maximum for the Pirates and as well as setting a new track record (albeit short-lived) for his 420-yard home strip, he had also been capped for his country. Poole used to present many awards to their riders in this era and at the close of the campaign Brian deservedly received the Freshmans Tankard for being the most improved novice of the year, while also scooping the Supporters' Club trophy for clocking the fastest time by a Pirate. What a season indeed!

Speedway, of course, was in Brian's blood and he really couldn't avoid becoming a rider. His father, Tom, had ridden for Exeter in 1947, and had he not tragically lost his life in a road accident at Christmas time that year, he would have been a member of Poole's promoting board along with Cliff Brewer, Herby Hayden and his own brother, Jack (or Johnnie as he was actually christened). In a further link, Jack Crutcher had two daughters and they both later got married to riders, namely Tony Lewis and Pete Smith. Brian's bikes were looked after and maintained by Poole mechanic Fred Wright, with much assistance from Norman Young, who for many years was the machine examiner at Wimborne Road and although now retired is still very active in the pits to this day.

Having won the Championship, the Pirates were promoted to Division Two in 1952 and they just kept on going in the same manner as they had the season before. Crutcher established himself as a heat-leader and it was little surprise that he topped the side's scoring, with 379 points giving him a league average of 9.68. One of his best performances, and there were many of them, was a scintillating full maximum (12) when the Pirates took Cradley Heath apart by 57 points to 27 on 6 October. Small wonder then that Poole took their

continued

second successive league title, finishing 8 points ahead of runners-up Coventry. Brian was presented with the Wessex trophy as the club's leading scorer, and on top of that he retained the Supporters' Club trophy for being the fastest Pirate – although he did have to share the award with Bill Holden.

Aside from his achievements with the team, his finest hour must have been qualifying for the World Final at Wembley on 18 September. He did it the hard way too, since being a Second Division rider he had to qualify from the first round. What a night it was for Poole Speedway as the fans turned out in force to support him, with many coaches in the car park proclaiming support for the 'Nipper'. Sporting the number thirteen race-jacket he first appeared in heat 4, when he finished in third place behind Dick Bradley and Split Waterman. Brian was straight out again in heat 5 and the cheers could surely have been heard in Dorset as he took victory from Jeff Lloyd and Graham Warren. After this promising start he was to land just 2 more points, but his total of 6 represented a great effort from one so young.

In 1953 he again lined up for Poole, but he didn't stay long. Having scored 86 points from 10 league matches, First Division Wembley came in with an offer for his services and since he had little more to learn from Division Two racing, he moved on to the famous Lions. The top-flight club paid a reported £2,500 for the rider, with Buster Brown also going to Poole as part of the deal. Brian was to add to his list of honours in a four-year stint with the Lions, during which he netted a total of 901½ points from 91 league matches and appeared in every World Final. His best season simply had to be 1954, when he scored 13 points to claim second position behind maximum-man Ronnie Moore in the World Championship, while on the domestic front he registered 10 maximums (9 full and 1 paid) on his way to 255½ points and a league average of 9.98. In terms of Division One racing he bettered that figure in 1956 when he finished fourth in the overall averages on 10.16, the top three being Barry Briggs (10.53), Ronnie Moore (10.44) and Ove Fundin (10.34), but he never again came so close to lifting the World crown.

Wembley closed down after the 1956 season and Crutcher moved to Southampton, where he remained a leading rider until the end of 1959, scoring a total of 565 league points for the club. He was non-riding reserve in the first two World finals whilst with the Saints, prior to signing off with a 10-point tally in what turned out to be his last big night at the Empire Stadium. Brian did sign to again ride for Southampton in 1960, but retired before the league programme began. He was still a young man, but the world of business beckoned. A truly brilliant and naturally gifted rider, he was one of England's greatest and arguably the best rider never to win a World Final.

Born: 10 November 1954, Oxford, Oxon

Competition	Matches	Points
League	65	512½
Knock-Out Cup	5	39
Others	48	428
Pirates total	118	979½

After practising in a field, John Harry Davis took his first proper speedway spins at Weymouth while still a schoolboy, and from day one his potential was clear to all who saw him in action. To gain experience he signed for Second Division Peterborough during 1971, making the long journey from his Dorset home each week accompanied by his father, Harry. He was to make excellent progress with the Panthers too, recording 53 points from 13 league matches for a 5.85 average. He was also called upon to help both Poole and Oxford in the First Division, actually making his Pirates debut in the side's first match of the season – a league encounter at Halifax on 27 March, when he netted a single point from two starts. He went on to total 4 league appearances in the blue and white colours, as well as riding in a couple of challenge matches, while for Oxford he rode in 3 Division One meetings.

The Peterborough promoter, Danny Dunton, who also promoted at Oxford, was pleased to welcome John back for a full season in 1972, and the youngster continued to climb the speedway ladder at a rapid rate, posting an 8.10 average, having registered 238 points from 30 league fixtures. He also raced in 10 matches for the then-nicknamed Rebels, and amongst the cut and thrust of the First Division he did well to attain an average of 3.10. Davis had a great year in 1973, making it to heat-leader status in Division Two, with an average of 8.95 for the Panthers, not to mention a healthy 6.19 figure when 'doubling-up' with Oxford. Aside from that, he had a couple of guest outings for Poole in the league, the best of which produced a return of 9+1 points in a home win against Newport on 25 July. Given his excellent record, unsurprisingly, Davis was to go full-time with the Rebels in 1974, when he accumulated 193 points to yield a 6.94 league average.

Much was expected from John the following year, but it wasn't to be with Oxford. He moved on to Reading, who were embarking on their first season of racing at their new Smallmead home. Bizarrely, while his move to the Racers was being ratified, he actually guested for himself in a league match for Oxford at Coventry on 22 March! With all the paperwork subsequently sorted out satisfactorily, he duly appeared in the opening meeting at Smallmead Stadium on 28 April, when his 8 points helped the Racers to defeat Hull 48-30 in a league encounter.

It was with Reading that Davis's career really took off, and in his first term with the club he raised his top-flight league average to 7.38. In all, he was to spend six full years with the Berkshire outfit, during which, he became possibly the most popular rider in

British racing. Much of the credit for this must go to the one and only Dave Lanning, who, while in charge of the fortunes of the Racers, did much to project the image of John. Whilst he was given lots of publicity, 'JD' still had to perform on the track, and this he did brilliantly. In 1976, he qualified for his first British Final, and although he never won the prestigious event, he was to amazingly make it through to a total of 16 finals. That same year he also posted a league average of 9.27, which he raised to 9.82 the following season when he also made it through to the World Final as reserve.

1978 saw a slight dip in form, but he was back with a bang in 1979 when he achieved a career best league average of 10.22. In 1980, John played a major part in Reading's League Championship success with 286 points and an average of 9.54, while on the individual front he raced in the World Final at Gothenburg, scoring a creditable 9 points. Although he began a seventh term with Reading in 1981, he sought pastures new and a mid-season move saw him link with Poole for a reported £20,000 fee.

John had continued to guest for the Pirates on numerous occasions during his years with the Racers, but what was his first outing as a fully-fledged Poole team member took place on 5 August when he netted 8+1 points in a 46-32 league victory over Sheffield at Wimborne Road. It wasn't long before JD netted a full-house for the Dorseteers, and this he did with great gusto when registering 12 points in a 42-36 defeat at Birmingham on 21 August. The following month, he hit a really purple patch, scoring maximums in 3 successive league matches. The first was a 12-point tally in a 50-28 win at home to Wimbledon on 9 September, and he followed that up a day later by helping himself to a 15-point haul in the return match against the Dons as Poole collected a 41-37 victory. Then, on 18 September, his contribution of a dozen points was instrumental in the Pirates' 42-36 success at Hackney. With form like that, Davis went on to top Poole's league averages on a 9.70 figure, having accrued 144 points from 15 matches.

Although not quite as dominant in 1982, he was the model of consistency on his way to retaining his position as the leading Pirate, with 193½ league points equating to an 8.76 average. Regrettably, despite his efforts and those of team-mate Scott Autrey, Poole finished at the foot of the British League standings, and it would be fair to say that the duo lacked the necessary support in the top-end scoring department. In 1983, John was second heat-leader to new signing Michael Lee and between them the pair formed a potent spearhead. However, towards the end of the season, Davis became a little restless and he was eventually loaned to Sheffield, having scored 109 points from 17 league matches. JD made a further 6 league appearances as he saw the campaign out with the South Yorkshire side, before another move in 1984 saw him identified with Wimbledon. He was to remain ever-present over the 30-match league programme for the Dons and in scoring 252 points, he achieved an 8.39 average. The year also saw him take one last outing in the blue and white colours of Poole on 22 August, when he guested in a home league match against Cradley Heath, but he enjoyed no luck on the night and scored only a single point.

With Wimbledon opting for National League racing in 1985, John found himself back at Reading and he was to add three more years of excellent service to his previous time with the Berkshire outfit. A further change of track then saw him link with King's Lynn in 1988, and although he began the following season with the Norfolk side, a switch in July took him to Swindon. During his late-season stint, he was to prove a steady scorer for the Robins and the Blunsdon faithful hoped he would remain on board in 1990. This he did, and from time to time, he came up with flashes of vintage form on the way to a total of 124 league points and an average of 6.62.

By the time March 1991 came around, JD had moved on again, with a return trip to Wimbledon. Upon the amalgamation of the leagues, the Dons had opted to join Division One, but a loss of money forced them to close in June, with the team relocating to Eastbourne. John was initially part of the new set up in East Sussex but he never really settled, and shortly after suffering a groin injury

he made up his mind to retire. However, an injury-hit Swindon stepped in to revive his career, and in a short stint, he did extremely well for the Robins, netting 70 points for a league average of 8.47.

Davis again lined up for Swindon in 1992, but after a bright start he suffered a bad leg injury in a Gold Cup match at Arena-Essex on 24 April, and unfortunately that was to bring the curtain down on a sparkling career. During John's time in the saddle, numerous England caps came his way and an obvious highlight was being part of the national side which took victory in the World Team Cup Final at Wroclaw, Poland, in 1977. He also made a second appearance in the World Final proper at Vojens, Denmark, in 1988, and in a meeting won by Erik Gundersen, he tallied 3 points. After his retirement, he became a successful businessman, but still maintained a keen interest in the sport and in recent years has acted as mentor and confidant to young English ace Lee Richardson.

Born: 6 November 1940, Hoyland, Norway

Competition	Matches	Points
League	35	330
Knock-Out Cup	I	II
Others	6	59
Four-team tournaments	I	10
Pirates total	**43**	**410**

Flame-haired Norwegian Reidar Eide took his first speedway steps in his homeland at Bryne, near Sandnes in 1957. Having made good progress he broke into the Stavanger side in 1960, but it wasn't until 1966 that British supporters really became aware of him. That was when he came over to assist Edinburgh and, showing great promise, he recorded 96 points from 19 British League matches for an encouraging 5.87 average. He was to enjoy a long career on these shores, during which he represented a number of sides and became renowned as a prolific points gatherer.

Reidar came on a bundle in 1967 and many terrific showings saw him rise through the ranks to the position of a heat-leader. Indeed, with 324 points from 35 matches, his average of 9.01 placed him just behind Swedish ace Bernt Persson (9.13) in the Monarchs' league statistics. Late in the year he really left his mark on the Poole supporters when, on 16 August, he swept to a 15-point maximum to win the High Speed Gas Trophy at Wimborne

Road. Then, on 20 September, against a quality field, he reeled off another 5-ride full-house to triumph in the Johnny Thomson Memorial Trophy. The year also saw him crowned as Norwegian Champion for the first time, and remarkably he was to go on and retain the title for five successive years (1967-1971).

Edinburgh shifted their home base to Coatbridge in 1968, and with a league average of 9.14 the Norwegian again finished as runner-up to Bernt Persson (9.58) in the club's scoring. What turned out to be his one and only World Final appearance occurred at Gothenburg on 6 September that year, but on the big night he could only attain 3 points, despite being expected to fare considerably better. With Persson moving on to Cradley Heath in 1969, Eide took over as the Monarchs' top man, plundering 336 points from 32 matches for a league average of precisely 10.00.

The Scottish side's track licence was subsequently taken over by Trevor Redmond and Bernard Cottrell in 1970, enabling speedway to return to Wembley. Together with some of his team-mates, Reidar relocated to the famous London venue and celebrated by becoming the Lions out and out number one with an average of 9.11, courtesy of 346 points from a full quota of 36 league matches. At the end of the season, he moved on to link with Poole after reaching an agreement with the Knott family, who were the promoters at the Dorset raceway.

Having previously shown a penchant for the 380-yard circuit, he was to have an excellent season representing the Skull and Crossbones. He made an inauspicious start in his club debut, however, scoring just 5 points in a league match at Halifax on 27 March. That proved only to be a temporary blip and he soon slipped into a consistently high-scoring groove thereafter. In fact he was so good that he shot straight to the top of the Pirates' league averages, with 330 points yielding a figure of 9.11. Such was his dominance that he finished way ahead of the next two riders in line, namely Odd Fossengen and Pete Smith, both of whom posted identical averages of 7.86. During the year, he revealed quite a turn of pace, and went through a record-breaking spree with the Poole track record. This began on 2 June, when he lowered the best time to 68.0 seconds in the opening heat of a league match against Exeter. Three weeks later, on 23 June, he equalled his own best time for the circuit in the first heat of a league encounter with Oxford, and then on 7 July, he established an even better time of 67.8 seconds in heat 1 of a league fixture with Newport. Unfortunately for the Pirates' supporters, Eide was on his travels again in 1972 and the many disappointed Wimborne Road patrons wondered just how he could possibly be replaced. The shrewd Poole bosses had the situation weighed up though, and came up trumps by signing Swedish thrill-merchant Christer Lofqvist.

Meanwhile, Sheffield was the speedy Norwegian's next port of call and he ended the campaign with a slightly reduced league average of 8.80 for the South Yorkshire club. After that, he moved to Newport in 1973 and simply had a ball in a three-year stint with the Welsh outfit, scoring 816 points from 87 league matches, topping their averages in 1973 and finishing second to the great Phil Crump in both 1974 and 1975.

The wanderlust then struck yet again and Reidar was next identified with Leicester in 1976, but his season ended abruptly in August when he suffered a double leg fracture in the Norwegian Championship. At the time, he had ridden in 23 British League Division One matches and, despite a number of mechanical problems, had still accumulated 185 points for a solid 7.92 average. After missing a huge chunk of the 1977 season, Eide finally made his return to the track with Leicester on 3 September. However, he was far from fully fit and this was reflected by the fact that he could only post a league average of 3.24, having registered 16 points from 6 matches.

Raring to go again in 1978, the Norwegian was part of a deal that saw John Titman join Leicester from Exeter, while he headed in the opposite direction to the Devon outfit. He was immediately back amongst the points and appeared at home on the pacy County Ground circuit as he supplied great backing to the Falcons' number one Scott Autrey. By the end of the season, Reidar had raised his average to 8.40, having racked up 233 points from 32 league fixtures. Yet another change of scenery saw him move on to Reading in 1979, but after starting reasonably well, he broke a leg in a French grass-track meeting and was absent throughout July, August and September while he recuperated. He found the going tough upon his late-season return and it was little surprise that his average slumped to 4.70 from a total of 16 league matches.

1980 was to be his last term in British racing and he bowed out by riding for no less than four different teams over the course of the season. After starting at Reading, he had equally short spells with Swindon and Eastbourne, before seeing out the year with Wolverhampton. Thankfully, he managed to avoid the injury bug and having attained a 7.08 league average for the West Midlanders, he announced his retirement to become Norway's national coach. Numerous stories suggested that Eide struck a hard bargain when it came to negotiating terms during his time in the saddle, but it has to be said he was the complete professional and gave of his best for all the sides he represented. Sadly, it was reported in February 1999 that Reidar had died, aged just fifty-eight. He had apparently been working as a pig farmer in Thailand and developed brucellosis, a fever which only farmers generally suffer from. Having flown back to his native land for treatment, he unfortunately slipped into a coma and passed away some two months later.

Born: 23 November 1960, Maywood, California, USA

Competition	Matches	Points
League	31	200
Knock-Out Cup	1	5
Others	29	207
Pirates total	61	412

Christened Guy Allen Ermolenko, this most popular of American racers has always been known by his family nickname of Sam. Born to parents of Russian descent, he first got into bikes at the age of fifteen, when he rode moto-cross. However, a bad accident on an ordinary road machine a year later meant he was absent from the motorcycle scene for a considerable time while he recovered. It wasn't until the back end of 1981 that Ermolenko took his first speedway rides and one of his early recollec-tions is of four-times World Champion Barry Briggs making an off-the-cuff suggestion that he call himself the 'Mad Russian' in order to ensure he got rides at the famous Costa Mesa circuit, where there were often more riders attending than there was time for practice!

An important step in Sam's racing career sub-sequently occurred after he had watched the 1982 World Final, held at the Memorial Coliseum in Los Angeles. Brian Maidment, the Poole co-promoter, spotted Sam in action, although it wasn't until September 1983 that he telephoned and invited the American racer to try his luck across the water in England. Albeit very late on in the season, Ermolenko duly arrived on these shores and went straight into the Poole side for a challenge match against Reading at Wimborne Road on 28 September. He was to score a single point from 4 rides in a 39-39 draw, but at least a start had been made on his British career and one that would go on to span over two decades, despite him already being nearly twenty-three years of age! Sam went on to represent the Pirates in 4 league fix-tures, scoring 15 points for an average of 4.25, and a sign of what was to come occurred in a home challenge match versus Cradley Heath on 26 October, when he netted 7+2 points in fine style.

Back with the Pirates right from the start in 1984, Ermolenko began the season with a bang! Poole opened with a challenge match against a Phil Crump Select side on 21 March, and while Michael Lee led the Dorseteers to a 45-32 success with a 12-point full-house, Sam was busy helping himself to a wonderful paid maximum (11+1). After that, he continued to make his presence felt, although naturally there were matches when his form dipped a bit; after all, it was his first full season in this coun-try and he was seeing most of the away tracks for the first time. There were some real top-drawer performances, however, not least in a British League match at Newcastle on 25 June. The Pirates were soundly beaten 50-28, but Ermolenko came up with the goods to register 14 points on the tight Brough Park track, only losing out on a maximum in the final heat when beaten by Joe Owen. At the end of a lengthy season, which finally ended with the Poole Traders' Gala Night on 4 November, Sam had chalked up 169 points from 26 league matches for a satisfactory 6.71 average. He missed the domestic season in 1985, although he did make one sensational appearance at Bradford on 31 August for the occasion of the World Championship Final. It was his debut in the sport's premier event and he raced to a tally of 13 points to tie at the sharp end of the leader board with Erik Gundersen and Hans Nielsen. That, of course, necessitated a title run-off, which was subsequently won by Gundersen from Nielsen, with Ermolenko having to settle for third spot – but a fabulous podium position nevertheless.

After such a terrific showing, 'Sudden Sam', as he was dubbed, just had to return to British racing in 1986 and thus began a long love affair with Wolverhampton. He was to represent the Wolves for ten successive seasons, during which he made 255 league appearances and scored 3,236 points. Two years in particular stood out with the West Midlands outfit, the first being in 1991, when he scored 305 points and topped the entire Division One averages with a figure of 10.74. Then, in 1993, the flying American went even better to record a mammoth 575 points and an average of 11.26, as he again led the way at the head of the First Division scoring stakes. In the interests of the sport, Ermolenko has always been happy to race elsewhere if Wolverhampton couldn't accommodate him. As such, he moved about a bit in his later years, scoring freely for Sheffield (1996), Belle Vue (1997), Wolverhampton (1998), Hull (1999), Wolverhampton (2000-2001), Belle Vue (2002) and back again at Wolverhampton (2003-2004).

Sam has overcome several horrific injuries during his career, the like of which would have seen many other riders quit the sport, but his determination to succeed has been an inspiration to many. Perhaps the worst injury occurred in the World Long-track semi-final at Herxheim, West Germany on 16 July 1989,

when he was involved in a horrific crash, breaking his right leg, his nose and also a wrist.

The achievements of the ace racer deserved to fill a book of their own, and indeed they did in 2003, when Brian Burford produced an excellent publication entitled *Breaking the Limits*. Looking down a long list of honours, Ermolenko reached the old-style World Final on a total of 8 occasions and was also a regular in the Grand Prix series of 1995 and 1996. The obvious highlight on the individual stage was being crowned World Champion at Pocking, Germany, on 29 August 1993. He represented America on numerous occasions and helped his country to 4 World Team Cup victories (1990, 1992, 1993 and 1998, the last as non-riding reserve), as well as a victory in the World Pairs Championship (1992). On the domestic front, Sam was twice a victor in the Division One Riders' Championship (1991 and 1994), and once also won the retitled Premier League Riders' Championship (1996). A measure of his enduring popularity with the Poole supporters was there for all to see when Sudden Sam visited Wimborne Road with his Wolverhampton side for an Elite League match on 25 June 2003. Before the meeting, he was available to sign copies of his book and suffice to say he was kept busy for ages as the Poole public paid homage to a former favourite. Also in 2003, on 24 July to be precise, he once more donned the Skull and Crossbones breastplate as a guest for an away league fixture at Ipswich. Match reporter Elvin King wrote in the *Speedway Star*: 'Sam displayed vintage form' and this was quite correct, since he powered to a faultless paid maximum (16+2 points) and helped the Pirates to a 51-39 success. Poole co-promoter Matt Ford, in offering congratulations, described him as: 'The perfect guest.' Well, you can't do much better than a full-house can you? What a rider and what a glorious career!

Born: 27 February 1945, Nes, Norway

Competition	Matches	Points
League	208	1,415
Knock-Out Cup	14	70
Others	42	276
Pirates total	264	1,761

It would be fair to say that the Poole promoters took a chance when they signed Odd Fossengen in 1968, but the Norwegian grasped the opportunity and never let the club down. The management and supporters had been confident their side would do well, especially with stylish Swede Gote Nordin again leading the attack as he had done so brilliantly the season before. Indeed, Nordin began the league campaign in fine fettle, racing to a paid maximum in a 45-32 victory over Wimbledon at Wimborne Road on 17 April. However, there was a shock in store when Gote announced he was quitting British speedway and returning to his homeland to take up a business position within the ESO company.

The Poole bosses looked around for a replacement and came up with two names, those of Czech international Antonin Kasper and the then-unknown Norwegian Odd Fossengen. Both were invited for trials and a photograph of Kasper sporting the Skull and Crossbones race-jacket even appeared in the speedway magazines of the time. Despite this, it was Fossengen who impressed the devoted Poole public, for although he was lacking in experience, his 'never-say-die' spirit made him a real hit. So popular was he that when it seemed likely he would be sent on his way home, the faithful supporters made it clear to the promoters by every means possible, including demonstrations, that the man they wanted was Fossengen. Those in charge listened, duly signed the 'unknown' and didn't regret it for one moment. It may seem a remarkable story but it is true and Odd went on the repay everyone's faith with an exceptional first year in Britain. Fair enough, he wasn't a Nordin in the scoring sense, but he did show the makings of a very fine rider as he plundered 238 points from 34 league matches for an average of 7.13. Many times the close bond he had forged with the fans was emphasized by a special war-cry that reverberated around the terraces, thus: 'Oddie, Oddie, Oddie – rah, rah, rah!'

International honours came his way, with a 5-point tally being gleaned in the Nordic-British Final, whilst in the World Pairs Final he partnered Oyvind Berg and helped his country to third place on the podium, scoring 11 points. Naturally, he was kept on board for the 1969 season, which turned out to be a truly memorable one for the speed merchants bearing the blue and white colours of the Pirates. With 26 wins and a draw from their 36-match league programme, Poole claimed the Division One Championship by 6 points from second-placed Belle Vue. Fossengen again made 34 league appearances and upped his scoring a tad to glean 248 points for an average of 7.69. That was sufficient to make him the side's third heat-leader, behind Pete Smith (9.52) and skipper Geoff Mudge (9.01). With two men boasting such high averages to spearhead the team there was no pressure on the popular Odd at all and he continued to serve up thrills in his own special way. There were a number of notable performances, including one against visiting Swindon in a league match on 23 April when, after a quiet start, he raced to a paid dozen points (11+1) in a 48-29 victory. Then there was a score of 10 points in another home win over Exeter on 2 July and, on the subject of the boys from Devon, many still recall a narrow 40-38 success at the County Ground just twelve days later when he netted 13+1 points. On the international front he raced for his country against Scotland, while individually he tallied just 2 points in the Nordic Final.

The Norwegian was again included in the Poole septet in 1970, and while he didn't make the sort of progress that many felt he should, he remained amazingly consistent as he recorded 245 points from a full quota of 36 league matches for a 7.57 average. In the World Championship, he again rode in the Nordic Final and a 7-point tally was to prove a career best at that level of competition.

For a fourth successive season he wore the colours of the Pirates in 1971, when his level of performance was as solid as ever. A total of 263 points flowed from his wheels for a league average of 7.86, and as far as statistics go this was to be his best year for the club. On the international scene he represented his country against Sweden and also rode in the qualifying round of the World Team Cup, when he scored 5 points. Back again in Dorset for the 1972 campaign, Fossengen tried as hard as ever, although to the surprise of many his average dropped a little. It wasn't that significant a dip though, as he totalled 183 points in league racing for a final figure of 6.69. He did, however, ride for the combined Norway/Denmark side

during the season, racing in matches against Australia, England, New Zealand and Sweden.

Happily, Odd was back on song in 1973, when, having registered 208 points his league average increased back up to 7.27. Once again he was capped for the Norway/Denmark combination, making appearances against a variety of nations, namely England, New Zealand, Poland, the Soviet Union and Sweden. He will have no doubt wanted to forget his showing in the Nordic Final, however, as he ended the meeting point-less.

The 1974 season came along and regrettably it was one that saw the end of the mega-popular Norwegian's racing career. The Pirates were riding in a Spring Gold Cup fixture at Oxford on 9 May, and on a track made difficult by persistent rain Fossengen tangled with fellow countryman Ulf Lovaas in heat 3, suffering a broken thigh after crashing down awkwardly. It was a bad injury and having had the thighbone pinned, he was out of action not only for the rest of the season but for the whole of 1975 as well. At the time of the injury he had appeared in just 5 league matches, scoring 30 points for an average of 6.10. With the pin subsequently removed in 1976, hopes of a track comeback unfortunately didn't materialise and he was lost to the sport.

Odd's link with Dorset did continue in his private life, since he had married a local girl and every so often he returns to the county, usually when on holiday, and never fails to pop into Poole Speedway. He is always afforded a warm welcome, with many folk still holding fond memories of his time in their colours. It was reporter Colin Smith of the *Evening Echo* who in 1969 described him as having a thrilling and colourful track technique. Few fans down Poole way would disagree with that comment and from a club that is renowned for the support of its riders, there is no doubting that Odd Fossengen can be considered a gem amongst gems.

Born: 17 March 1930, West Ham, London

Competition	Matches	Points
League	104	896
Knock-Out Cup	6	54
Others	19	159
Four-team tournaments	1	0
Pirates total	**130**	**1,109**

Ronald Genz had an interest in racing on two wheels from an early age and as a youth he participated in cycle speedway. Such was his proficiency at the discipline that he was actually crowned East London Champion, and it was obvious that he would one day become a speedway rider proper. While he completed his national service with the Army, he continued to straddle a machine as a dispatch rider and in 1949, like many would-be riders before him, Ronnie began training at the famous Rye House circuit.

In 1950 he signed for New Cross, who at the time were in the First Division of the old National League. He rode mostly in second-half events and junior matches, but his persistence was rewarded when he broke into the senior Rangers side for a home league encounter against West Ham on 16 August. He might have only scored a single point, but it was a mark on the speedway ladder. He was

to ride in a further 5 league matches before the season ended, but he failed to add to the point he registered in his first match. Promoter Fred Mockford realised the youngster needed extra rides at a lower level to further his learning curve, so he loaned him out to Third Division Wolverhampton in 1951. Genz benefited no end from this, knocking-up 60 points in league racing for the then nicknamed Wasps. One match took him to Poole on 8 October, when he scored just a single point, but little did the Pirates supporters realise that they were watching a rider who some fourteen years later would be allocated to them by the Rider Control Committee as a heat-leader for their first season in the newly-formed British League!

Despite the fact Wolverhampton would like to have retained Ronnie's services for 1952, he returned to New Cross and rode in 29 league matches, totalling 69 points for an average of 4.10. Despite his progress, he was surprisingly loaned out to Second Division Yarmouth in 1953, but there was a shock in June when Fred Mockford closed down New Cross due to falling attendances. Genz, however, was making strides up at the 'Bloater Pond' and ended the league campaign with 105 points to his name.

In 1954, he was still to be found in Division Two, although a change of home track took him to Oxford, and thus began a long association with the Cheetahs that initially was to last until 1964. He won his very first race in the colours of Oxford and went on to accrue 149 league points to occupy second place in the club's scoring, behind Peter Robinson (172). He was to become a consistently high scorer in Second Division circles over the next two years, netting tallies of 249 and 279 points in 1955 and 1956 respectively.

With so few tracks left running in 1957, Genz, and Oxford, found themselves in an eleven-team National League, but it didn't seem to have any adverse affect on the rider, since he kept on doing the business to rack up 171 points and fill top spot in his side's list of league contributors. During the 1958 campaign he suffererd an eye injury which was to trouble him for some time, and he underwent an operation the following year. This naturally meant he was absent from a number of matches in both seasons, but nevertheless he still finished with respective league totals of 109 points in 1958, and 94 in 1959.

The 1960s dawned and Ronnie continued on his merry way, accumulating a further 632½ points over a five-year spell, thereby taking his career total to 1,683½ in an eleven-season stint for the Cheetahs. Looking at 1964 in a little more detail, it was a difficult time for the sport, as the stronger Provincial League ran outside the jurisdiction of the Speedway Control Board. Oxford had remained in the National League, and under the new promotional duo of Rodney Rycroft and Cyril Melville the Cheetahs swept to the Championship and also scooped both the National Trophy and Britannia Shield. There was one strange thing which happened to Genz along the way, when he made an appearance for Exeter in the Provincial League, riding under the assumed name of 'Reg Neal'. He was caught red-handed and subsequently fined £5 for the offence.

After his loyalty to Oxford, 'Genno' was moved away to Poole under the Rider Control system, which had been formed to help with the equalisation of team strengths. These days, Ronnie would have most certainly qualified for a Testimonial, but such things didn't happen in 1965, Despite this, he was more than happy to join the 'Pirate Ship', and in truth it is likely that a new challenge in a brand new set-up was just what he needed. Poole made a great start to the new British League era, winning 40-38 at Wolverhampton on 9 April, and then securing a 39-39 draw at Swindon the following evening. Genz scored 8 points against the Wolves and went one better versus the Robins, but there was plenty more to come. On 16 April

Poole entertained Exeter in an Easter Trophy encounter and the Pirates supporters were on cloud nine as their side claimed a 44-34 success, with the added bonus of the new recruit flying to a 12-point maximum on what was his home debut. On 22 April Poole visited Oxford for a league fixture and, from a Cheetahs' point of view, it must have been strange to see their former favourite sporting the colours of the opposition. Rubbing salt into their wounds, Ronnie scored 11 points and led his new team to a 44-34 victory, with his maximum only being scotched by a superb effort from Arne Pander in heat 5.

The Londoner quickly settled to life at Wimborne Road and his consistent scoring made him an immediate hit with the Dorset shale supporters. On 23 June, Poole hosted a World Championship qualifying round, and riding at the top of his form, Genz sped to victory with a fabulous 15-point full-house. The success saw him go through to the British Final at West Ham on 31 August, accompanied by team-mate Bill Andrew, but unluckily Ronnie suffered an ankle injury in the big event and could only manage a single point. In spite of the knock, he was straight back in action for the Pirates and the points simply flowed from him and his smooth-running machinery. At the end of the term, he had remained everpresent throughout Poole's 34-match league programme and a total of 332 points yielded an average of 9.58. Indeed, such was his form that he topped the club's figures and proudly wore their blue and white colours at the Belle Vue-staged British League Riders' Championship on 16 October. However, Genz enjoyed no luck on the big night and he could only manage a couple of points.

Back with the Pirates in 1966, he put together another fine season, although he was displaced in the number one position by Bill Andrew. Whenever speedway buffs mentioned Ronnie, he was always, quite rightly, referred to as dependable. It summed him up beautifully and, emphasising this, his figures for the year were 300 points from 35 matches for a league average of 8.83. He embarked on a third term with Poole in 1968, and despite slipping down to third place in the club's figures, he still totalled 264 points for an 8.03 league average.

He again got the 'lot' (15) to triumph in a World Championship qualifier at Wimborne Road on 17 May, proving, as he often did, that when in the groove, he was the master of the circuit.

To the disappointment of the Poole patrons, Rider Control struck at the beginning of 1968, posting 'Genno' back to Oxford. He was to head the Cheetahs' scoring but, having netted 229 points, he crashed at Cradley Heath on 31 August in what was his 27th league match of the campaign. Unluckily, he sustained head injuries and severe concussion, the combination of which was sufficient to rule him out for the rest of the year. He bravely tried to make a comeback in 1969, but was far from fit, so left it until 1970 for a track return. Understandably, it took him time to find his feet, but he manfully battled on to register 239

points from 35 league fixtures. In 1971, he did his bit for an Oxford side that was in serious need of strengthening, but after he had completed 20 league matches, Rider Control stepped in and allocated Tommy Roper to the Cheetahs, while Ronnie was posted off to Newport. Although he did his best for the Wasps, he decided to retire after 13 matches had produced a league average of just 4.38.

Ronnie Genz and riders like him were the reason that Rider Control worked. Whenever he was moved, he did it in good grace and gave of his best for the team he was allocated to. However, it would have been nice to think he could have remained with Poole in 1968, for he did enjoy his spell as a Pirate under the promotion of the Knott family, and it clearly showed in three seasons of excellent on-track effort.

Born: 2 February 1933, Ayton, nr Eyemouth

Competition	Matches	Points
League	127	1,077
Knock-Out Cup	10	155
Others	54	469
Three- and four-team tournaments	5	46
Pirates total	**196**	**1,707**

Although Ross Gilbertson was Scottish-born, it was actually at the picturesque California-in-England circuit that speedway folk first became aware of his name, when he appeared for the Poppies in Southern Area League action. This was in 1954, and although he only managed to accrue 7 league points during that first year in the sport, at least a start had been made to his 'shale-shifting' career. The league, although small in numbers, gave valuable opportunities to novices and Ross was to develop in 1955, ending the season with an increased tally of 45 points for California.

With the Northamptonshire venue of Brafield failing to open in 1956, the Southern Area League was reduced to just three sides, but to keep it competitive a fourth team, called Southern Rovers, was formed. Despite having no track of their own, they made temporary use of other venues for their 'home' fixtures, with one such meeting taking place at Swindon on 25 August. As usual, Ross was in the Poppies' line-up and he enjoyed a terrific meeting to net 9+2 points, only missing out on a paid maximum when beaten by Colin Gooddy in heat 8. Although California went on to end the campaign in the wooden spoon position, the young Scotsman had made much progress, totalling 83 points and finishing just behind the club's leading scorer Peter Mould (86).

Due to the call for Sunday observance, the Poppies moved to Aldershot for the 1957 season and Ross took the change of home circuit in his stride, rising to the number one position in the scoring stakes with 89 points. In 1958, Vic Gooden took over the Poole promotion, and the formation of a Junior League gave the lad from Ayton his first opportunity in the colours of the Skull and Crossbones. The Poole

Juniors first took to the track in a home match against their counterparts from Swindon on 21 April and won a thriller of a meeting 31-28, with Gilbertson recording 5+1 points. That was to be his only meeting for the side, however, as the Junior League petered out and many of the fixtures were not completed. This was a great pity, especially as Vic Gooden had entered the Poole side in an effort to help the league get established. In 1959, speedway tried again, with both the National Reserve League and the Southern Area League supplying young riders with chances to learn. Ross was to represent two teams, scoring 14 points for Oxford in the former mentioned league and 23 points for Eastbourne in the latter.

So to 1960 and the formation of the Provincial League, which not only proved a godsend for Ross Gilbertson, but also for many others speedsters like him. Cynics referred to it as a 'comeback' league, but it gave a valuable opportunity for riders to gain experience and make good. Gilbertson was duly snapped up by Poole, who were pioneers of the new racing division under the promotion of Charles Knott Snr. This had an added advantage for Ross, as he was also given extra rides with Mr Knott's 'senior' side, Southampton, in the National League. As things turned out, he was to score 20 league points for the Saints, but it was for Poole that he really shone. In notching 134 points over the course of the league programme, he was the Pirates' top man, leading the way from Ken Middleditch and Geoff Mudge. In fact, Gilbertson enjoyed quite a season, since he set a new track record time of 72.0 seconds in the Vic Gooden Trophy versus Rayleigh at Wimborne Road on 22 June. Additionally, he rode in open meetings at his old home base of Eastbourne, where he enjoyed a glorious treble, winning the Easter Trophy, the Southern Area Riders' Championship and the Supporters' Trophy. Further lengthening his amazing list of individual successes for the year, he also carried off the Stadium Trophy at Rye House as well as scooping the Heal Trophy at Bristol. A popular innovation to the Provincial League was the Silver Sash Match Race Championship and Ross had a short reign as the holder, defeating both Reg Fearman and Ray Harris, before losing out to Doug Templeton. Completing the story of a wonderful term, he rode as reserve in the Provincial League Riders' Championship at Cradley Heath, recording a 3-point tally.

Poole were only just pipped to the league title by Rayleigh in 1960, but they were to go all the way in 1961, winning the Championship by a 7-point margin from Plymouth. In accumulating 188 league points, Gilbertson was one of three excellent heat-leaders who led the Pirates challenge, along with Ken Middleditch and Tony Lewis. His tally placed him third in the club's scoring, although it would have been sufficient to make him the number one rider at eight of the other ten teams in the Provincial League. Aside from his fine riding for Poole, he again regularly visited Eastbourne, where he gleaned another triple success, winning the Championship of Sussex, the Silver Helmet and the Supporters' Trophy.

In 1962, the Pirates retained the League Championship ahead of Neath, and although Ross suffered from niggling injuries, he still managed to register 149 points from league

matches alone. True, his tally had dipped a trifle over the year, but when 1963 came along, he was back to his brilliant best, gathering a terrific total of 240 league points to head the club's scorechart for a second time. One outstanding highlight occurred on 14 August, when he established a new track record time for the 380-yard Wimborne Road circuit. This was a special attempt to beat the clock, but it had actually been totally unscheduled. The Pirates had been due to face Newcastle in a league match, but three members of the Diamonds team were delayed following a road traffic accident in the New Forest. Promoter Charles Knott arranged impromptu entertainment while the large crowd waited for the Newcastle team members to arrive, including four attempts at the track record, of which Gilbertson's time of 69.2 seconds was the quickest. Incidentally, the three visiting riders eventually arrived and after beginning almost an hour and a half late, Poole swept to a 51-27 success. To close the season, Ross appeared in the Provincial League Riders' Championship at Belle Vue on 28 September. He did well too, scoring 9 points and then claiming a spot in the grand final after taking second place in a dramatic five-man run-off. The Poole representative didn't make the best of starts in the final though, and ultimately had to settle for third position behind winner Ivan Mauger and Jack Kitchen, but nevertheless it was a very fine achievement indeed.

As is well-known, the Provincial League rode 'black' in 1964, but Gilbertson again lined up for the Pirates. The team had a poor year by their terrifically high standards, finishing sixth out of twelve sides. Ross was a solid as ever, however, plundering 152 points from the league programme and finishing as runner-up to skipper Geoff Mudge in the club's scoring. The season also saw him rocket around the Poole raceway to equal his own track record in the opening heat of the Johnny Thomson Memorial Trophy on 3 June. Although his time of 69.2 seconds was subsequently equalled by both Barry Briggs and Gote Nordin, the record was to stand until 21 June 1967, when it was finally bettered by Ivan Mauger.

Following a 'marriage' between the National and Provincial Leagues, the British League was born in 1965, and Ross began yet another season with the Pirates. He did well in the new set-up, riding as consistently as ever to card 212 points from 31 matches for a league average of 7.84. During the year, he secured his first cap for Scotland against Russia at Edinburgh on 10 July, scoring 4 points. Although seemingly at the peak of his powers, Gilbertson surprised everyone when he decided to retire at the end of the season in order to concentrate on building up his business interests.

In 1969, he was tempted out of retirement to join the newly-formed Romford team in the Second Division, and he revealed all his old sparkle, racking up 305 points for a huge 9.98 league average. Another season followed with the Bombers, before he finally quit the sport for good after being identified with Canterbury (1971-1973) and Eastbourne (1973). He had served speedway well and worked his way up from the Southern Area League to the British League by sheer hard work. He was one of many riders who welcomed the extra rides of the Provincial League in 1960, and was a star in that sphere right from its inception. After retirement, Ross continued to be a regular at Poole, watching his favourite team in action, although unfortunately he hasn't enjoyed the best of health in recent times.

Colin Gooddy

Born: 25 June 1933, Blackheath, Surrey

Competition	Matches	Points
League	134	549
Knock-Out Cup	17	62
Others	29	117
Four-team tournaments	4	131
Pirates total	184	741

Colin William Gooddy began racing on motorised bikes following a successful time as a cycle speedway rider during which he not only represented Blackheath and New Cross, but also earned caps for England. Affectionately known as 'Joe' throughout his career in speedway, he originally started with odd outings at Aldershot in 1951 and it wasn't until 1978, when a Poole rider, that he finally announced his retirement. Indeed, it was remarkable that his time in the saddle spanned such a long period, since in those early days of 1951 he actually retired after some rather unproductive second-half rides. Little was heard of him until 1954, when he resurfaced for practice at Brafield. The following year saw Colin net 40 points, as he managed to hold down a place in the Flying Foxes side in the Southern Area League.

He was on the move in 1956, linking with Southern Rovers – a team with no home circuit of their own, who simply rode wherever other promoters would allow them some track time. One such meeting was held at Swindon on 25 August, when Joe recorded 7 points as his Rovers team beat California 42-41 in a thrilling encounter. Continuing to hone his skills, he enjoyed a good year with the 'homeless' side, ending the term wth a tally of 81 points in league racing.

In 1957, the Rovers were based permanently at Rayleigh and Gooddy was a valued member of the team. However, he was keen to ride for

Eastbourne and an eventual rider exchange saw Leo McAuliffe join the Rovers, with Colin going in the opposite direction to the Arlington-based club. Unluckily, he was injured shortly after his dream move, but not before he had recorded 28 points for the Eagles on top of the 27 he had previously carded for Rayleigh.

Joe was certainly moving around to further his experience and in 1958, he was identified with Yarmouth in the Junior League. The league was ill-fated, with many fixtures not completed, and the Norfolk outfit closed down at a time when Gooddy had recorded a total of 14 points. The season wasn't a complete disaster though, as he enjoyed some rides with National League Oxford at what was the beginning of a long and happy association with the university city club.

It was back to Eastbourne in 1959, when he topped the league scorers, but his link with Oxford was still in evidence too, and in a successful campaign he registered 61 National League points for the Cheetahs, plus 77 in the Southern Area League for the Eagles.

In 1960, Colin started the season with Oxford, but having netted 16 league points, he soon found himself on the way to Ipswich, with Jack Biggs heading the other way as part of the deal. Joe was to score 50 points for the Witches in league racing, and remaining with the Suffolk side in 1961, he recorded another 93 points and was one of the successes in a team which finished in sixth spot. 1962 came along and Gooddy was riding well for Ipswich, but support was poor and the track closed down in mid-season. Colin, who had scored 93 league points at the time, returned again to Oxford, where he was to provide great service up to and including 1964 – a season when the Cheetahs won a glorious treble of the National League Championship, National Trophy and Britannia Shield.

During his latest two-and-a-half-year stint with the club, he accumulated another 228 points in league activity, his best return being a tally of 116 in 1963. The National League, however, had been dying on its feet and was down to just seven teams. This situation could not go on and was addressed with the formation of the British League in 1965, when the Rider Control Committee tried to post Joe to Long Eaton. The rider wasn't keen on the idea and eventually moved to Exeter, where he simply loved the sweeping bends of the 433-yard County Ground raceway. Indeed, he remained ever-present over the 34-match league programme and became the Falcons' number one, with 322 points yielding a high 9.20 average. During the year Colin made a first appearance in the colours of Poole, when he rode as a guest in a challenge match at King's Lynn on 23 October, recording a 7-point tally.

A drop in figures saw him slip to third position in Exeter's scoring stakes in 1966, but he still notched 241½ points for a 7.21 league average. He stayed with the Falcons until partway through the 1967 season, when a disagreement with the management saw him once more return to Oxford. At the time of his departure, he had ridden in 13 league matches, scoring 77 points for an average of 6.78. The move back to Cowley did him a power of good and in 19 meetings he registered 149 points and raised his league average back up to 8.51. Gooddy was then an Oxford regular right the way through from 1968 to the end of 1972, during which he made a further 169 league appearances and totted up 1,028½ points.

A year with Cradley Heath followed in 1973, when he scored 126 points from 28 league matches for a 4.97 average. Given the statistics and the fact that he had turned forty years of age, it really came as a surprise when Charles Knott brought him to Poole in 1974. However, being very shrewd, Mr Knott knew what he was doing. He wanted a 'back-up' man for his side and, in Colin, he got exactly that. The evergreen rider gained a new lease of life on the Dorset coast, emphasised fully by a haul of 168 points from 29 league matches.

In 1975, Malcolm Simmons was recruited by the Pirates, and although Joe's scoring dipped slightly to 111 points, he still posted a useful 5.43 league average. Perhaps his finest performance of the year occurred in a home match versus Hackney Wick on 4 June, when he raced through the card to hit a 12-point full-house. Still at Wimborne Road in 1976, his season began badly when he suffered a broken collarbone in a challenge match against a touring Poland side on 21 April. He wasn't out of the saddle for long though and was as reliable as ever in achieving a league figure of exactly 5.00 from 33 matches.

During the 2003 season, many riders in Britain were 'doubling-up' or indeed, 'doubling-down', but this practice was by no means new, since in 1977, Gooddy, who was frequently referred to as the oldest rider in top-flight racing, also turned out for Crayford in the National League. It proved to be a tremendous term for him as he garnered 251 points for the Kestrels for a league average of 8.58, while for the Pirates, a tally of 125 points produced a figure of 5.51. Due to his dependability and sheer zest for the sport, he was named as rider of the year at Poole. He may not have hit many high scores for the boys in blue and white, but he always rode as if his very life depended on it. No wonder the generous Poole crowd loved him.

Having reached the veteran stage, he was again associated with Poole in 1978, his Testimonial year, but he was dogged by knocks and suffered serious back injuries on two occasions. Having recorded 36 points in the league, he wisely called it a day. His much-deserved Testimonial meeting duly took place at Eastbourne on 8 October, when the Pirates claimed a 47-42 success over the Eagles in a grand challenge match befitting of the occasion. Joe Gooddy represented all that speedway is about. He was reliable, always worked hard for his points, never gave up trying and was an inspiration to his younger team-mates. He was a no-nonsense rider who wasn't afraid to speak his mind and say what he thought. As such, you always knew exactly where you stood with him and there's absolutely nothing wrong with that. These days, he enjoys his retirement at home near Blandford Forum in Dorset.

Born: 18 February 1971, Drammen, Norway

Competition	Matches	Points
League	240	2,131
Knock-Out Cup	29	231
Others	36	311
Three- and four-team tournaments	19	131
Pirates total	**324**	**2,804**

Lars Gunnestad was an ultra-keen thirteen-year-old when he began racing on 80cc speedway machines in Sweden, and he clearly enjoyed the experience as he spent some considerable time perfecting his technique. Having stepped up to 500cc bikes, such was his progress and outstanding ability that he was crowned Norwegian Champion in 1988 at the tender age of seventeen. Since Lars had done much of his training in Sweden, it was only natural that he raced in their version of the Elite League and he was to have a long association with Indianerna. In 1990, he grabbed a second national title and also qualified for the final of the World Junior Championship, held at Lvov in the Soviet Union on 9 September. The line-up for the big event featured several riders who went on to great things, including winner Chris Louis and the third-placed Tony Rickardsson, with Lars putting on a great show to net 9 points and finish in sixth spot.

Continuing on the up, Gunnestad duly completed a hat-trick of Norwegian titles in 1991 and in the World Pairs Final at Poznan, Poland, he and partner Einar Kyllingstad rode out of

their skins to claim an excellent third position on the podium. These successes ensured that Lars was closely monitored by British promoters, and sure enough he was invited over by Sheffield promoter Cliff Carr to join the Second Division outfit for a late-season stint.

His debut occurred in an inter-league challenge match against visiting Berwick on 29 August and he made a good start for the Tigers, collecting 2 race wins on his way to a total of 8+1 points. He went on to represent Sheffield in 6 league matches and greatly impressed in scoring 68 points for an 8.50 average. Clearly, he needed to move into top-flight racing and, after missing the UK season in 1992, a year when he retained his country's national crown, he was snapped up by Poole in 1993. Thus began an excellent relationship between club and rider, with Gunnestad first sporting a Pirates race bib in a Division One match at Cradley Heath on 27 March. In a closely fought match, Poole went down to a 56-52 defeat, but it was the form of the new recruit in the number six jacket that caught the eye, as he showed a fair old turn of speed to record an excellent 10 points. Lars was to enjoy his first year in the top-flight, producing many splendid displays along the way, not least when he posted a paid maximum (14+1 points) in a league fixture versus Ipswich at Wimborne Road on 18 August. Come the end of the season, he had landed another Norwegian title, while for the Pirates he made 37 league appearances, scoring 309 points for an average of 6.93.

His all-action style and ready smile made him a huge hit with the Poole supporters and he was welcomed back in 1994, when he rose up the ranks to heat-leader status. Double-figure tallies became a regular feature on the Pirates' scorechart until his season ended abruptly in September, when he took a hefty knock to a knee in the Norwegian Championship. At the time, Gunnestad had registered 293 points to yield an 8.83 average from 29 league meetings. The year also saw him triumph at the first attempt in Poole's prestigious Blue Riband individual event on 3 August, when, having totalled 11 points he swooped from behind to win the final from Jason Crump, Craig Boyce and Steve Schofield.

Fit again in 1995, Lars plundered 376 league points for a high 9.94 average and, with the aforementioned Crump (who averaged 10.41), formed a potent spearhead for the Pirates. His list of achievements grew longer when he won a second successive Blue Riband, and to cap a fine year he also became Champion of Norway for a sixth time. He continued to score heavily for Poole in 1996, when he accrued 425 points to average 9.09 in the league, while on the individual front, he remarkably scooped a third straight Blue Riband victory.

Regrettably in 1997, Gunnestad was to miss out on the chance of equalling Malcolm Simmons' record of 4 Blue Riband wins on the trot, as he packed up his kit and returned home prior to the event's rearranged date of 22 October, after it had been rained-off two weeks previously. For the Pirates, his league form took a step backwards and he finished with a 7.45 average, although he was obviously affected by his father's ill health at the time.

Unfortunately, Lars was but a shadow of his former self in 1998 and after struggling to find his touch he eventually asked to be dropped, with Gary Havelock being brought into the Poole side as his replacement. With 118 league points and an average of 5.47 to his name, he had slipped to a reserve berth and unsurprisingly he was to remain at home in 1999. He did at least have the consolation of winning the Norwegian Championship in both 1998 and 1999, making him an 8-times holder of the title.

Gunnestad made a popular return to the 'Pirate Ship' in 2000, however, when he looked much more comfortable in accumulating 199 points for a 7.29 league average. Lars was still on board with the Dorset side in 2001, his Testimonial year, but the season had only just got underway when he suffered a broken leg and jarred a shoulder while riding for Rybnik in a Polish First Division match at Opole. Although quickly back in the saddle, the shoulder injury was to affect his movement and it wasn't until August that he was able to score freely.

Having added another Norwegian Championship to his long list, his Testimonial meeting took place at Wimborne Road on 29 August, when the generous Poole fans turned out in force to pay tribute to a grand club servant. A four-team tournament was the order of the day and, fittingly, Gunnestad led his Scandinavian Select side to victory in an entertainment-packed event. Before the meeting, he was honoured with the royal gift of Kongepokal (the King's Trophy) in recognition of his 9 Norwegian title successes. This was awarded by King Harald V of Norway and is the highest accolade that a sports person can receive in his country. Finishing the campaign with a flurry, Lars was to end up with a league average of 6.06, having tallied 127 points.

This mega-popular rider didn't figure in the Pirates' team plans for 2002 but, following an injury to Grzegorz Walasek, he came in to make 6 end-of-term league appearances for a 6.48 average. With further Craven Shield, Play-Off and challenge match outings, he took his career total to 2,804 points in the cause of the Skull and Crossbones, giving him a top ten place in the club's all-time scoring list. He missed the 2003 season on these shores, but he wasn't idle and amazingly managed to plunder a 10th Norwegian Championship. Having also ridden in the World Long-track Final and taken several wildcard outings in the Grand Prix over the years, Lars' achievements are many, but throughout it all he has remained the same friendly-natured chap and you couldn't wish to meet a nicer fellow.

Born: 4 November 1968, Yarm, Cleveland

Competition	Matches	Points
League	116	901
Knock-Out Cup	13	103
Others	40	295
Three-team tournaments	5	31
Pirates total	174	1,330

Robert Gary Havelock was always likely to take up a career in speedway, since his father, Brian, was a leading rider during the 1970s and early 1980s, riding for a number of Second Division/National League teams in the north of England. Gary in fact had his first motor-bike at the age of just three and progressed on to the junior grass-track scene five years later. At the age of fourteen, he started attending speedway training schools, where he was a 'star' pupil, always listening and willing to put good advice into practice. By the time 1985 came along, he was more than ready to stake a claim for a place in his local team, Middlesbrough, and duly made his debut on 28 March, scoring 7 points in a challenge match versus Long Eaton at Cleveland Park.

Once in the Tigers' side he went from strength-to-strength to post an impressive National League average of 7.27, having accumulated 205 points from 33 matches. Opportunities also came his way in top-flight racing with King's Lynn and Wolverhampton, and the young 'Havvy' was quite rightly described as one of the finds of the season.

He moved up to the role of a heat-leader with Middlesbrough in 1986, lending tremendous support at the top-end to Martin Dixon and Mark Courtney, as his league average rose to 8.55. He was to show sparkling form in the British League as well, making 13 appearances for Bradford and yielding an average of 7.43. It was only natural that the West Yorkshire out-fit would want Havelock on a full-time basis in 1987 and he was happy to step-up in the fur-therance of his career. Having signed for the Dukes, he was to remain loyal to the club until the end of the 1997 campaign, when they regrettably closed their doors to speedway after winning the inaugural Elite League Championship. During that time, Gary did miss the entire 1989 season, having been banned by the Speedway Control Board after a drugs test had proved positive at the previous season's British League Riders' Championship, held at Belle Vue on 9 October. It has to be said that although he was aged only twenty at the time of the ban, he took his punishment like a man and returned in 1990 an even better rider.

He was to become an international regular for England, but there was one particular per-formance that really made his name and this occurred at the Olympic Stadium in Wroclaw, Poland, on 29 August 1992. The occasion was the World Final and Havelock took his bow in the sport's premier event, and what a debut it was too! He showed grit and determination to take the title with a 14-point tally, losing only to Pole Slawomir Drabik in a rerun 8th heat. Due to heavy rainfall, track conditions were poor and Gary also injured an ankle in the orig-inal running of heat 8, but if these caused problems to him no one would have known, as he powered his way to the crown.

In his long association with Bradford, he took his total of league appearances for the club to exactly 300, from which he recorded 3,210½ points, his best term occurring in 1995 when he posted a huge 10.32 average. His long service to the Dukes was rewarded with a Testimonial meeting on 8 June 1997, when a large Odsal attendance witnessed him lead his side, the North, to a 50-40 win over the South.

There was another feature of his game that had developed during his time with Bradford and that was the art of both team riding and captaincy. Indeed, Havvy was excellent at motivating his colleagues, giving plenty of encouragement and always trying to help his partner when out on the track. With the Bradford riders made available for transfer by promoters Bobby and Allan Ham, it was something of a surprise when Gary linked with Eastbourne in 1998. It was a long way from his northern base, but he was well organised and regularly raced abroad, so the travelling did not bother him. Unfortunately, and not through any lack of trying, he found it difficult to get to grips with the Arlington raceway, and in a late-season switch he joined Poole, where he replaced an off-form Lars Gunnestad. To a degree, he was taking a chance with the move, since he could not have had good memories of the Wimborne Road circuit. This dated back to 3 July 1996 when, riding for England against Australia, he suffered serious back injuries in a track accident and was out of action for the remainder of the season. Anyway, he had already guested for Poole earlier in the year on 10 June, when he scored 2 points in a league match at King's Lynn, but happily, having become a fully-fledged Pirate, he celebrated by recording a tally of 9+1 in a home encounter versus Oxford on 19 August. With his season kick-started, Havelock was to bag 82 points from 9 league matches (including the guest outing) and was a 'must' for a team spot the following year.

In 1999, Matt Ford and Mike Golding became co-promoters at Poole alongside Pete Ansell, and an enthusiastic Havvy displayed vintage form as the Pirates finished second in the Elite League, just a single point behind Peterborough following a dramatic end to the Championship chase. An inspirational skipper, he stayed ever-present throughout the 18-match league programme to register 156 points and an average of 8.64. That average slipped a little to 7.72 in 2000, when, over an extended league schedule of 32 matches, he accrued a total of 241 points. Despite that, Gary was still a highly valued member of the Poole set-up, with his leadership qualities much appreciated by management and fans alike.

Riding with more consistency in 2001, he was able to record 232 points from 29 matches for an increased league average of 8.06. Backing the top two of Tony Rickardsson and speedy Pole Krzysztof Cegielski, he helped the Pirates to challenge for the league title, although in the end, as in 1999, they narrowly missed out, finishing a point behind Champions Oxford. They did have the consolation of winning the Craven Shield, however, with success in the three-legged final gained against Peterborough and Wolverhampton. Such was Havelock's form during the year that he managed to rejuvenate an international career which had been 'on hold' for some time. This occurred when Pirates' boss and national team manager Neil Middleditch brought him back into the fold for Great Britain in matches against Australia and Denmark, prior to making him captain for the Speedway World Cup tournament in Poland.

2002 was to be Gary's last term with Poole and his season was to end prematurely when he sustained a broken arm in a home match versus King's Lynn on 26 August. Prior to that, a series of niggling mechanical problems had seen his league average drop to 6.82, although he remained as popular as ever at Wimborne Road for his 100 per cent efforts. The Poole bosses restructured their side in 2003, unfortunately with no place for Gary, and he subsequently moved on to Peterborough, where he has remained for 2004. Aside from his World Championship glory in 1992, Havvy also rode in the 1993 final and appeared in the Grand Prix series of 1995 and 1996. Other individual successes in a glittering career included winning the British Under-21 Championship (1986), the British Championship (1991 and 1992) and the Premier League Riders' Championship (1995).

Born: 1918, Bournemouth, Dorset

Competition	Matches	Points
League	147	717
National Trophy	14	79
Others	39	220
Three- and four-team tournaments	2	0
Pirates total	202	1,016

Charlie Hayden was one of a small body of men who worked ceaselessly to ensure the formation of Poole Speedway. Prior to that, both Charlie and his brother Herby had been well known on the grass-track scene, being members of the Ringwood Club. In 1947, a number of Bournemouth-based riders signed for Exeter Speedway, these being Charlie, together with Sid Hazzard, Tom Crutcher and Alan Chambers. On 14 April, all four took part in a meeting entitled as a 'Battle for Team Places' at the County Ground circuit, and it was certainly memorable for Charlie, since he came out on top with an 11-point tally. Interestingly, all the races were started on the green light, as a new starting gate hadn't yet arrived at the Devon venue! Although he remained in the Falcons squad after that impressive start, he wasn't a regular team member and at the end of the season, he was credited with just 18 league points.

The Bournemouth boys hoped that one day the cinder sport would be staged locally, and although the town's Kings Park had been mooted as a possible home, the idea came to nothing. However, in January 1948, Poole Council accepted an offer of £1,000 per annum

for a ten-year lease at a site on Wimborne Road, and the rest, as they say, is history. Sadly, Tom Crutcher never saw the venture come to fruition, as he lost his life in a motor accident, but Messrs Hayden, Chambers and Hazzard all lined up for the newly formed Pirates in their very first match, a Division Three encounter at Tamworth on 14 April. Charlie skippered the side and scored 4 points, but couldn't prevent the Hounds from thundering to a 63-21 victory.

Poole's first home meeting took place on 26 April and pitched them against Great Yarmouth in a National Trophy tie. In a very unfortunate start, Hayden was involved in an accident on the first bend of the opening race, when visiting rider Reg Craven had engine trouble and poor Charlie couldn't avoid running into him. The Pirates captain suffered concussion, but recovered sufficiently to race in the return match the following day. Tragically, the news wasn't so good for Reg Craven, who had received severe head injuries and passed away eight days later. Hayden duly netted 13+1 points in the second leg at Great Yarmouth, his efforts helping Poole to gain an aggregate success, but the events of that first race at Wimborne Road had understandably affected him. After racing in league matches against Hull (home), Hastings (away) and Southampton (home), plus both legs of a National Trophy tie with Hanley, he took a break from speedway and resigned the captaincy, the job passing to Joe Bowkis. He subsequently returned to action in a reserve berth at Wombwell on 2 July, recording 3 points in a heavy 56-28 defeat and really hit the highs shortly afterwards on 19 July, ironically when Great Yarmouth returned to

Wimborne Road for a league match. The Pirates went on the rampage to win 60-23, with their former skipper showing his best form to construct a quite beautiful 12-point maximum.

Given the times, it was quite something for Poole to be invited on a short tour of Sweden in October, when they raced in 3 matches. Charlie's best meeting of the trip occurred at Eskilstuna, where he scored 5 points in a 30-30 draw. He undoubtedly rendered yeoman service to the club throughout the season, and at the end of the campaign had accumulated 137 points from 29 league matches.

In 1949, Hayden enjoyed himself as a regular in the Poole team, producing a number of excellent performances on his home circuit. There were several good returns, including 10+1 points against Liverpool on 18 April, 11 points versus Halifax on 9 May, when he lost only to Vic Emms in the opening heat, and 10 points against Hull on 30 May. Then, on 3 June, he plundered an 11-point tally at Leicester, being beaten by Cyril Page in heat 10, when a slight overslide allowed the Hunter to pass and ruin his maximum in the process. By the season's end, Charlie had accrued 230 points and ridden in all but one of the Pirates' 48 league matches, missing just a home match against Great Yarmouth on 15 August after sustaining a wrist injury.

In 1950, after an indifferent start results-wise, Poole signed Ken Middleditch from the defunct Hastings, and really began to take off. Hayden played his part with several notable showings, including 11 points at his old Exeter home on 4 August, when the Pirates forced a 42-42 draw. That same month, the men bearing Skull and Crossbones bibs raced at the pear-shaped Aldershot raceway and came away with a 52-31 victory under their belts, Charlie's contribution being another magical 11 points. Finishing off a term of consistent scoring, he recorded 11 points against Liverpool in a home match on 25 September, taking his overall tally to 179½ points from 35 league meetings. Having lost ground at the beginning of the season, Poole recovered well to eventually end the campaign as runners-up to Oxford in the Third Division table, thanks largely to the big scoring of Cyril Quick, Ken

Middleditch and Dick Howard. As one of the back-up boys, Hayden, together with team-mates Tony Lewis, Ticker James and Terry Small, was described as 'sound, without being sensational' in the *Stenners* report of the year, which was a fair comment indeed.

The 1951 season was one to savour for supporters of the Pirates. A change of promotional staff brought in Geoffrey Bravery and Len Matchan, two ambitious local businessmen, who were never afraid of spending money to strengthen the team. Their combined efforts paid dividends, with Poole storming to the Division Three Championship ahead of Exeter. They boasted a powerful side, and with a number of riders at the top end, Charlie was simply able to ride to the best of his abilities without any added pressure. As such, he rode in every one of the Pirates' 36 league matches and totted up 170½ points for a solid 6.55 average. Highlights were 10-point returns in home matches against Long Eaton and Wolverhampton on 11 June and 16 July respectively. His generally good form was recognised internationally on 6 September, when he was called-up to ride for England 'C' versus the USA at Wimborne Road, and he celebrated by scoring 5 points.

Poole were promoted to the Second Division in 1952, but the move up a flight did not appeal to Hayden. He subsequently relocated to Wolverhampton, where his Poole boss Len Matchan had become co-promoter. Although Charlie was also joined at Monmore Green by his old Pirates team-mate Cyril Quick, by and large he struggled to find form and having recorded 64½ league points, he tried his luck with St Austell. His fortunes did not really improve in the Cornish side, although he did have one good night at Swindon on 23 August, when he carded 9 points, only for his side to lose narrowly 43-41. For the Gulls, he totalled 51 points in league racing, before calling it a day at the end of the season. He continued to support the sport following his retirement, and Poole Speedway owes much to Charlie and his brother Herby, whose hard work in the early days helped hasten the shale sport's arrival in the coastal town.

Born: 4 January 1918, Bournemouth, Dorset

Competition	Matches	Points
League	24	50
National Trophy	4	19
Pirates total	**28**	**69**

Sidney Hazzard first became prominent on the grass-track scene, and after turning his attentions to speedway he initially gained experience on the cinders at Bristol. Along with a small group of other Bournemouth-based riders, he simply couldn't wait until the sport was introduced locally. Prior to that, in 1947, whilst plans to stage speedway at Poole unfolded, Sid and his colleagues were signed up to ride for Exeter in the new Third Division of the National League. It is important in the history of Poole Speedway to remember just who those pioneers were, for in addtion to Sid, there were the Hayden brothers, Charlie and Herby, along with Alan Chambers and Tom Crutcher.

Nicknamed 'Hap' for obvious reasons, Sid is recalled as a real thrill-maker at Exeter. Indeed, the Falcons manager, Frank 'Buster' Buckland, was so impressed with his penchant for using the County Ground's solid steel safety fence to drive off the bends that he offered him £5 if he could get his rear wheel up on the surround. The story goes that Sid did in fact do something a bit special on one occasion, actually getting both wheels to momentarily mount the fence and returning home with an extra tenner in his pocket for his efforts! At the end of the season, he had racked up a total of

95 points in league racing and provided much in the way of excitement for the Exeter faithful. However, with Poole ready to go in 1948, he naturally wanted to race for his local side and a fee of £60 was said to have changed hands to bring him to Wimborne Road.

His debut duly took place in the Pirates' first match at Tamworth on 14 April, but in an inauspicious start for both rider and club, he recorded only a single point as Poole lost the league encounter 63-21. The great day of the Pirates' opening home meeting dawned on 26 April, when Great Yarmouth provided the opposition for a National Trophy match. Proudly sporting the Skull and Crossbones race-jacket, Hazzard went into the history books as one of the riders who took part in the very first heat. To be fair, it wasn't scheduled that way, since Sid was programmed at reserve, but as is well known, the first attempt to run the race saw the visiting Reg Craven suffer engine trouble, with Poole skipper Charlie Hayden unavoidably running into him. Both men came down, with Alf Elliott, the other Pirates representative, doing a tremendous job in laying his bike down to avoid the fallen riders. Reg Craven was taken to hospital, where he tragically succumbed to his injuries eight days later, while Charlie Hayden was forced out of the meeting with concussion. Thus, it was Hazzard who replaced Hayden in the rerun, and he went on to finish second to the Bloaters' Paddy Hammond, who set the first track record of 83.6 seconds. Poole went on to swamp their opponents 74-32, with Sid unbeaten by an opponent for the rest of the meeting, as he raced to a fabulous tally of 12+2 points from 5 outings.

Sid's harum-scarum riding style certainly won the hearts of the Poole public, but it meant he was prone to injury and he did spend periods on the sidelines as a result. When fit, several on-track performances stood out, particularly when Hull came to Wimborne Road for a league meeting on 3 May. Hazzard ended the night with 6+3 points to his name, and could quite easily have recorded a paid maximum had Hull's George Craig not caused him to fall in heat 6. The Angels rider was excluded, but Sid was a trifle shaken and as such was unable to take part in the rerun. A couple of other good nights occurred later in the season, the first of which saw him net 7+1 points in a fine 51-31 home win over Hanley on 6 September. Then, four days later, the Pirates went down narrowly 43-40 at Wombwell and 'Hap' enjoyed his best-ever away showing for the club, scoring another 7+1 points. Looking through the record books, he must have had a liking for the big 443-yard South Yorkshire raceway, since he had registered 8 points for Exeter when they had visited on 16 May the previous year.

At the end of Poole's first campaign, the statistics showed he had ridden in 24 league matches, posting a total of 50 points. These weren't the sort of figures he wanted, and that, coupled with the injuries he had sus-

tained, influenced his decision to hang up his racing gear.

Having retired from active racing, Sid became team manager of the Pirates, and later, following a change of promoters, he moved on to Plymouth, where he was put in charge of both the workshops and the Devils side. Always a loyal man, he didn't forget his old friends amongst the Poole riders, and when the Dorseteers management made changes that left lads without a club, he was always pleased to offer them trials at Plymouth. Frank Wheeler and Frank Holcombe were two such ex-Pirates who raced for the Devon outfit, the former doing particularly well in 1951, totalling 78 league points. A most interesting man to converse with, Sid was always pleased to discuss one of his favourite subjects, that of speedway. He happily kept in touch with his old racing colleagues and there wasn't much he didn't know about the sport, or indeed its sister activity of grass-track racing. Like a number of his former team-mates, he realised his dream of seeing speedway at Poole, and the club's success over the years, must have been a source of tremendous satisfaction.

Frank Holcombe

Born: November 1919, Bournemouth, Dorset

Competition	Matches	Points
League	67	159
National Trophy	4	14
Others	7	16
Three-team tournaments	1	1
Pirates total	**79**	**190**

Ernest Frank Holcombe was interested in motorcycles from an early age and actually acquired his first machine at the age of eleven. Later, he and brother Doug took a real liking to grass-track racing, which was particularly popular in the Southern Centre. Frank was a member of the Ringwood Club, whose home circuit was located at the Mount in Poulner, and he was described as one of the leading riders in the area.

Moving on to the birth of speedway in Poole, the part played by the Holcombe family simply cannot be underestimated. Indeed, Mr Holcombe Snr helped with the track laying, putting his skills as a road builder to very good use. Perhaps the most amazing thing, however, was that the Pirates nickname was actually hatched in the front room of the Holcombe family home, being suggested by Frank himself to the Hayden brothers, Charlie and Herby, upon one of their visits to discuss the ongoing developments at Wimborne Road.

Given his considerable experience on grass, it wasn't surprising that Frank applied for trials at the new cinder track. Having suitably impressed, he appeared in the opening meeting on 26 April 1948, when, following Poole's 74-32 victory over Great Yarmouth in a National Trophy tie, he defeated fellow grass-trackers Bingley Cree, Dink Philpotts and Jock Pope in the second-half Junior Race. His winning time of 92.6 seconds, remarkably, wasn't the slowest of the meeting, since Joe Bowkis had been timed at 107 seconds dead in heat 13 of the main match! It is worth remembering that the circuit was 420 yards in length at the time, with deep cinders as the racing surface and the first track record established was in fact 83.6 seconds.

Holcombe didn't have to wait long before making his debut for the Pirates in a league match at home to Wombwell on 24 May, when he sported the number eight race-jacket. He was first called into action in heat 8 as a replacement for Joe Bowkis, who had been excluded for breaking the tapes. He did a grand job too, splitting the tough visiting pairing of Harwood Pike and Harry Welch to claim a highly creditable second place. He only took one further outing that night, when running a last in heat 12, but no matter, he had made a start to his career as a Pirate.

Things generally proved tough for the newcomer, but there was a bright spot when Hanley travelled down to Dorset for a Third Division fixture on 6 September. Poole were dealt a blow in heat 3, when they lost the services of both Alf Elliott and Charlie Hayden following an overslide by visiting Potter Vic Pitcher. This meant their programmed rides had to be covered by Frank and fellow reserve

Sid Hazzard, with the duo subsequently performing heroically to compensate for their missing team-mates. After a couple of third-place finishes behind his partner, Holcombe brilliantly followed Alan Chambers home for a 5-1 in heat 8, before crowning a superb showing by taking the flag ahead of Jack Dawson in heat 12. The Pirates went on to win 51-31, with Frank's contribution being a paid 10 points (7+3), while Hazzard netted 7+1. Another highlight occurred on the road shortly afterwards, when Holcombe tallied 7+1 points at Hull's 'D' shaped Hedon circiut in a league match on 11 September, his display including a heat 1 victory over Norman Johnson. Come the end of his initial season in the sport, he had totalled 56 points from 30 league matches and received plenty of encouragement from the loyal Poole public.

In 1949, he was a member of the Pirates team from the off, but one or two knocks were to cause losses in form and he endured a couple of stints on the sidelines. During the early part of the season, his best meeting was when Liverpool journeyed to the South Coast for a Division Three encounter on 18 April. In a 50-33 success, Frank's score of 6+2 points included partnering Cyril Quick to maximum points over Alex Gray in heat 10. Later in the season, after missing 3 league matches, he returned to the Poole octet and enjoyed a notable night on 27 June when he bagged 7+1 points in a home match versus Hastings. However, soon after that he was out of the side once more and missed a further 9 league matches.

He resumed in the side on 15 August and celebrated with a well-taken 7+1 points against Great Yarmouth at Wimborne Road. Mention must be made of the cruel luck Holcombe encountered when the Pirates entertained Exeter on 10 October. He was leading the opening race and on course for a new track record when he unfortunately fell and, while he remounted for a point, Exeter's Norman Clay went on to win in a time that equalled Ticker James' best for the circuit of 76.0 seconds. At the end of the campaign, he had accumulated 101 points from 36 league matches and, despite his problems, the figures represented considerable improvement on those of the previous term.

In 1950, Frank scored 2+1 points in the season's opening league match at home to Liverpool on 27 March, but that was to be his only outing for the Pirates all year. Aside from netting 7 points in the Cliff Brewer Trophy on 10 April, he then all but disappeared from the speedway scene until 1951. That was when old pal Sid Hazzard, who had moved on to the post of team manager at Plymouth, offered him rides. Things didn't go too well and he only recorded 19 league points for the Devils, which effectively brought a close to his racing days.

He remained heavily involved on the other side of the fence though, beavering away behind the scenes at Poole, tuning engines for the likes of Ken Middleditch, Tony Lewis and Johnny Thomson. Sadly, Thomson crashed in a home match against Ipswich in a National Trophy tie on 9 May 1955, fracturing his left femur, and after suffering an embolism he tragically died four days later in Poole General Hospital. This hit Frank hard, and as a mark of respect, he and his brother donated a Memorial Cup, which was first presented later that year on 11 July, after the Pirates had slaughtered Oxford 76-19 in a Second Division match. The trophy went to Bill Holden, whose winning time of 72.4 in heat 7 was the fastest recorded by a home man on the night. Meanwhile, on the back of the match programme from the meeting, Supporters' Club Honorary Secretary, Mrs. L.A. Harris explained that envelopes were to be distributed so that fans could contribute towards the purchase of the Johnny Thomson Memorial Shield. This was subsequently first raced for on 3 October 1955, and either as a second-half event or a full-blown meeting, it was run every year up to and including 1973.

No article on the career of Frank Holcombe and indeed his family, would be complete without some reference to his sister, Betty, who could strip down a speedway bike and build up an engine with the best of them. During the preparation of this book, the authors learned that Frank had sadly passed away at the age of eighty-four in November 2003. He certainly played his part in the history of Poole Speedway and he did have his moments around the Wimborne Road circuit, even though he didn't enjoy a great deal of luck.

Born: 8 March 1923, Blackburn, Lancashire

Competition	Matches	Points
League	174	1,225
National Trophy	40	273
Others	48	290
Four-team tournaments	2	15
Pirates total	**264**	**1,803**

Although Lancashire born, William Holden has been associated with Southampton for much of his life, and in fact still lives there to this day. During the winter of 1949/50, his speedway career began at a school held by Bob Oakley at the Hamble training track, situated within close proximity of Southampton. Bill, then a local taxi driver, was considered the top pupil at the school and there was further evidence of his talent when he plundered a 15-point maximum to triumph in the Future Stars Trophy at Southampton on 18 July 1950. As a result of his success, he won a contract with the Saints and following some useful second-half showings he was to go on and net a total of 16 points from 13 Division Two matches. Despite his low return, Holden displayed rich promise and all he needed was racing experience in order to develop into a fine rider.

Following a close season crammed with practice, he was in the Southampton side which entered the 1951 campaign. However, the crippling effects of Entertainment Tax led to promoter Jimmy Baxter withdrawing the Saints from the league in June. Bill was credited with scoring 20 points at the time and he subsequently sought rides at Poole in the furtherance of his career. On 25 June, after the

Pirates had defeated Swindon 48-36 in a Third Division encounter at Wimborne Road, he was programmed for a couple of second-half outings. He duly won the Stadium Scurry in great style, and in the Invitation Scratch Race he was again victorious, beating Frank Wheeler and the Swindon duo of Bob Jones and Danny Malone. It was therefore a noteworthy day for Holden on 3 July when he became a Poole rider and helped the Pirates to a 53-31 league success over Exeter, his 4-point tally including a tremendous win in heat 12.

Bill was used as a reserve in his early matches as a Pirate and he and sixteen-year-old sensation Brian Crutcher formed an outstanding partnership. Their most eye-catching performance together occurred in a Division Three match at Swindon on 7 July, when the Dorseteers went on the rampage to win 53-31. Holden's contribution was a wonderful paid maximum (11+1), while Crutcher was also unbeaten, scoring 8+1 points from 3 starts. Shortly after that, on 25 July, Bill equalled Ken Middleditch's track record of 72.8 seconds when he rocketed around the Poole raceway in a match against Aldershot. His superb riding was recognised internationally and 3 England 'C' caps came his way – two against New Zealand at Cardiff and Swindon, and one versus Sweden at Poole. Needless to say, the Lancastrian didn't stay at reserve for long and come the end of the season he had totted up 181 points from 26 matches in the cause of the Skull and Crossbones, giving him a highly impressive 8.24 league average.

Having swept to the Championship, Poole were promoted to Division Two in 1952, and for four seasons they really were the leading side in that particular sphere of the British racing scene. With little movement on the rider front, a fabulous team spirit was generated and things simply buzzed at Wimborne Road. Holden was a regular in the side throughout 1952, appearing in each and every one of the Pirates' 44 league matches to score 291 points for a 7.98 average. The Poole boys took the rise up a division in their stride, racing to the Championship in fine style by 8 clear points from Coventry. In a reversal of the positions, however, the Bees pipped Poole to the league title by a single point in 1953, although it's fair to say the Pirates would have surely lifted the Championship had Brian Crutcher not been transferred to Wembley after completing just 10 matches. Bill had another sound year, again remaining ever-present over the shortened league programme of 32 matches to register 193 points. A further cap came his way at Poole on 13 July, when he recorded 3 points for Britain versus the Overseas.

In 1954, Bristol were granted permission to drop down to the Second Division, and it was hardly surprising that they went on to scoop the Championship. Poole once more had to settle for the runner-up spot, but at least Holden enjoyed another excellent term, his total of 165 points placing him second only to Ken Middleditch (172½) in the club's league figures. The Pirates were renowned as excellent visitors, a fact which always ensured good crowds wherever they appeared. It wasn't quite the same story at home though, as summed up by distinguished journalist Peter Morrish, who commented that 'stronger opposition was needed [again] to attract customers.'

The 1955 season was probably Bill's best in the colours of Poole, and his backing of Ken Middleditch played a key role in the side's title success by an 8-point margin from Coventry. In superb fashion, Holden accumulated 319 points from 31 league meetings, but with the Pirates finally gaining a richly deserved promotion to the First Division, he didn't feel he would be competitive in the top-flight and requested a move. However, his bosses, and indeed the fans, had faith that he would be able to 'cut it' at the higher level. Having decided to try his luck, he did give it his best shot, but it didn't work out. Poole drafted in some riders with Division One experience and skipper Ken Middleditch raised

his game, but Bill and his team-mates from the Second Division days unfortunately found the going much too tough. Having recorded 53 points from 16 league matches for an average of 5.60, he finally got his wish and dropped back down to Second Division racing with his old club, Southampton. He soon settled down and generally looked much happier, scoring 75 league points for the Saints before the end of the season.

In 1957, there were so few teams left running that the First and Second Divisions amalgamated, and Holden again found himself amongst the elite with Southampton. This time around, he did well to accrue 103 National League points, thereby proving that he could in fact ride competitively against top-class opposition. Things went pear-shaped with the Saints in 1958 though and following a loss of form he was allowed to rejoin Poole. Regrettably, after making a reasonable start to life back with the Pirates in the Britannia Shield, he began to struggle and after scoring 23 points from 6 league matches, one of the best-ever riders to pull on the club's breast-plate retired from the sport he had served with excellence.

Born: 24 March 1922, Islington, London

Competition	Matches	Points
League	103	590
National Trophy	10	74
Others	37	208
Three- and four-team tournaments	3	14
Pirates total	**153**	**886**

Richard Howard became a speedway rider in the post-war period, when the sport was enjoying large crowds and training schools were springing up all over the place. His first skids took place in 1946 and, having gained additional experience through practice at West Ham, he was to briefly assist Birmingham in the Northern League, scoring just 2 points. The Third Division was subsequently formed in 1947 and the Londoner became a member of the Hanley side. Given the limited experience he had, his form was nothing short of sensational for the Potters as he piled up 151 league points to finish second in the club's scoring behind skipper Dave Anderson (180).

Remaining with the Staffordshire outfit in 1948, Dick was in the side that visited Poole for a Division Three fixture on 21 June. It wa not a meeting he would remember fondly, however, as the Pirates raced to a 45-36 victory and he netted only 3 points. The return match took place at Sun Street on 1 July, when Hanley turned the tables to triumph 53-31, with Howard enjoying a much better night in carding 9 points. Later in the season, Dick was loaned to Poole by the Hanley promotion to replace Joe Bowkis, who had been injured, somewhat ironically, when racing against Potter Gil Blake in the Third Division Match Race Championship. He subsequently made his debut as a Pirate on 27 September in a league match against Exeter at Wimborne Road and, sporting the number five race-jacket, he accrued 5 points. The match resulted in a massive 52-31 loss for Poole, but despite the heavy defeat, the evening was notable for a couple of reasons. The main talking point was the floodlighting, which illuminated the racing for the first time at Wimborne Road, but with rain in the air it was also the first occasion on which a home meeting was run in wet conditions.

Dick had two particularly good nights in his new colours before the season's end, both occurring in home league matches, with tallies of 8+3 points against Wombwell on 13 October and 8+2 versus Southampton on 25 October. Altogether, he accumulated 158 league points over the year, 123 of them for Hanley, with his 35 for Poole being gleaned from 7 matches.

Having joined full-time in 1949, he went on to become a firm favourite with the Poole public, not only for his all-action riding style, but also for his sense of fun. His take was that the crowd had come to be entertained and as such he never failed to give the fans value for money. Emphasising this was a home match against Hastings on 1 August, when he took a fall in his second ride and his bike actually ended up in two halves – a thing like that, the Poole supporters were sure, could only happen to Dickie!

The season was drawing to a close when he produced a marvellous performance against visiting Exeter on 10 October. The Devonians boasted three stylish heat-leaders in Norman Clay, Don Hardy and skipper Arthur Pilgrim, but in spite of the high-quality opposition, the match turned out to be a special triumph for Howard. He began with a heat 2 victory over speedy Australian Hugh Geddes and then took care of Clay in the fifth race. Again, he defeated Geddes in heat 8 for his third straight success and to complete a magical full-house he streaked clear of Hardy to win heat 11. The Pirates went on to register a 46-38 victory and eminent speedway correspondent Jim White commented: 'Dick Howard rode the match of his career and scored his first-ever maximum on cinders.'

At the end of the term, he had ridden in 45 league matches for 279 points, a total which placed him third in the team's scoring behind Cyril Quick (386½) and Fred Pawson (383). Mention of Pawson conjures memories of the superb team-riding when he and Dick were paired together. They seemed to have a terrific understanding of each other's style and their combined skills were very much appreciated by the Wimborne Road faithful.

Still with Poole in 1950, he was in great form when the side visited Oxford for a challenge match on 30 March. The Pirates lost 48-34, but with a 12-point maximum to his name, Howard was the undoubted star of the show. As things panned out, his performance was made all the more remarkable since the Cheetahs went on to claim the Third Division Championship.

Poole generally had a poor start to the season, but Dick rode as well as any of the lads who proudly bore the blue and white breast-plate. A maximum at Liverpool on 7 April, when the Pirates rode to a breathtaking 42-42 draw, showed that he was doing his utmost for the team. When Ken Middleditch joined Poole later in April, the fortunes of the side began to improve, with Howard providing valuable backing to the scores of both Ken and captain Cyril Quick. A short-lived claim to fame occurred in a Third Division match at home to St Austell on 24 April. Visiting rider Ken James established a new track record of 76.6 seconds in heat 2, only for Dick to lower it further to 76.2 in the tenth race. Not to be denied, James amazingly shaved the time down to 75.6 seconds in the second half, meaning Howard's record had lasted for about half-a-dozen races! As usual, he was always available for a bit of fun and when Tamworth journeyed to Dorset for a league match on 15 May, Dickie had the whole stadium of fans laughing fit to burst when he suddenly appeared at the pit gate with a huge pair of ladies bloomers. As one of the promoters at the time quipped: 'Dick certainly scared the pants off somebody!'

By the end of the campaign the Pirates had climbed up to the runner-up position in the Division Three table, finishing 5 points adrift of Champions Oxford. Howard remained ever-present throughout the 36-match league programme and, as with the previous year, he was again third in the list of Poole scorers, having attained 196 points. As with all statistics, the figures simply don't tell just how much effort went into his racing, but suffice it to say his contribution to the cause was greatly valued by the knowledgeable Poole supporters.

A new promoting team of Geoffrey Bravery and Len Matchan took over the reigns of the Pirates in 1951, and in the early stages of the campaign Dick did enough to hold down a team place. However, the new bosses were ambitious and when Second Division Southampton closed down after completing just 7 league matches, a couple of the Saints' riders were drafted into the Poole side, namely Bill Holden and Roy Craighead. Although he hadn't been riding badly, Howard was by and large left with second-half outings and eventually made an appearance for Division Two side Ashfield in a league match at Cradley Heath on 28 September. Dick had ridden in 15 league matches for the Pirates at the time he lost his team place, and had netted 80 points, but the management probably felt vindicated in the decisions they had made since Poole went on to win the Third Division Championship.

Howard began the 1952 campaign with Ashfield but, having accumulated 46 points from 17 league matches, he had a spell on the sidelines. He was later to ride in a First Division match for West Ham, prior to linking with

Wolverhampton in the Southern League. Len Matchan, his former boss at Poole, had joined the West Midlanders as co-promoter at the start of the season and Dick was duly signed on to assist the then-nicknamed Wasps. He did reasonably well to tally 41 points in league racing for Wolverhampton, but was on the move again in 1953, firstly riding for Plymouth and then Exeter. In league racing, he recorded 10 points for the Devils and 22 for the Falcons, before drifting out of the sport. However, in 1957 he briefly returned to Poole when the circuit hosted a series of open-licence meetings, having pulled out of league racing due to the effects of petrol rationing coupled with the unwanted expense of undertaking track alterations. He didn't have much luck though, and finished with the sport for good after scoring just 2 points in 3 matches.

Dickie lived locally and was a regular at Wimborne Road right up until his death, aged eighty-one, in March 2003. It is also worth mentioning that he was a bit of a crooner and during his days with the Pirates he often sang at Supporters' Club events and in his local pub. His favourite song was 'Red Sails in the Sunset' – a ditty made famous on the radio by comedienne Suzette Tarri.

Born: 23 November 1924, Bournemouth, Dorset

Competition	Matches	Points
League	63	332
National Trophy	6	40
Others	10	25
Three-team tournaments	1	10
Pirates total	80	407

Dennis Gordon James, always known as 'Ticker', initially started racing on the grass in 1948, but such was his progress that in a very short space of time he was having trials on the cinders at Southampton and Poole amongst other venues. Having impressed greatly at Wimborne Road he was subsequently signed by Poole and made his public debut on 20 September that year when, following a 46-38 league victory for the Pirates over Great Yarmouth, he appeared in the Dorset Scratch Race. He might have only run a third-place finish behind Frank Holcombe and Bingley Cree, but at least he had taken his first steps towards a team slot. He continued to plug away in second-half events and, on 4 October, he enjoyed a fruitful night, firstly winning his heat and then the final of the Dorset Scratch Race. As a result, he qualified for the final of the Stadium Scratch Race and despite taking a tumble on the first lap, he had done enough to be selected for the Poole side in their next home match versus Wombwell on 13 October.

Proudly sporting the Skull and Crossbones race-jacket, James duly came to the line for his opening ride in heat 4 and straight away the supporters were cheering when the new Pirate team-rode beautifully to follow home partner Alan Chambers for a 5-1. If that ride was good, then better was to come. The sixth race saw him link with Charlie Hayden on another maximum, but his *piece de resistance* undoubtedly occurred in heat 9. Things began badly when Ticker reared from the gate, hit the fence and appeared to be out of contention, but he somehow remained in control of his steed and set after the Wombwell duo of Red Hamley and Harwood Pike. With a high degree of skill,

and with the crowd excitedly roaring their approval, he picked off the Colliers duo to accompany Hayden on another maximum. Unbeaten by an opponent, James lined up for his final ride in heat 13, but with Charlie Oates producing a fine ride the new Pirate was foiled in his attempt to land a paid full-house. Still, with 8+3 points to his name, it had been a tremendous debut and he had played a full part in Poole's 58-26 success on the night. He was just as effective in a home encounter against Tamworth the following week and by the season's close he had taken his league total to 23 points from 4 matches.

James was a regular Pirates team member in 1949 when, week by week, he gradually progressed and developed into a real crowd favourite. During the season, he notched a 4-ride maximum (12) when the Pirates faced Swindon in a home league meeting on 5 September. Perhaps more notable was his outstanding performance a week later though, when Poole entertained Exeter, also in a Division Three match. The opening race saw Cyril Quick burn up the raceway to equal the track record of 76.4 seconds, but nobody was prepared for the incredible heat that followed. This saw James leave the tapes like a rocket and he had already established a 20-yard advantage from colleague Dick Howard as they exited the south bend. He increasingly pulled away to eventually win by half a lap and such was the pace he had set that nobody in the large audience was surprised upon learning he had set a new record of 76.0 seconds for the 420-yard circuit. No one could touch him on the night, as he went on to complete a fine 12-point maximum and led Poole to a 45-39 victory in the process. Extending his purple patch to three successive home maximums, he again ripped around the Wimborne Road track to notch a dozen points against Leicester on 19 September. He looked to be carrying on in the same vein when he won his first 2 rides against Tamworth one week later, but he came down heavily in heat 10 and was unfortunately ruled out of action for the remainder of the season.

Speedway was most definitely in the James family; Ticker's younger brother, Ken, became a fellow Pirate in 1949 before moving on to St Austell when the Cornish track joined the Third Division the following year. The statistics for the year showed Ticker had accumulated 156 points from 35 league matches and the loyal Dorset supporters hoped he would take on the role of a heat-leader in 1950. Unfortunately, illness caused him to miss the opening meetings of the campaign, and this, coupled with the fact that Fred Pawson had returned to parent club Harringay, was a contributory factor in the Pirates making an indifferent start to their programme. Happily, Ticker returned for a home league match versus St Austell on 24 April, and in the second heat he witnessed his brother clock 76.6 seconds to equal the track record then held by Cyril Quick. To quantify this, during the winter months the circuit had been relaid using red shale, and as such it had been decided to begin again from scratch with the track record! Later on, in heat 10, Dick Howard lowered the best time to 76.2 seconds, only for Ken James to go even faster in the second half when he was timed at 75.6 seconds! Just seven days later, on 1 May, it was Ticker's turn to break the track record, when he blasted around to win heat 9 of a challenge match against Oxford in 75.2 seconds. His form was excellent and further evidence of this was served up in a World Championship qualifying round at Rayleigh on 17 June, when he took victory with 13 points. He sailed through to the next round at Walthamstow but was sidelined after crashing down in the opening heat at the East London venue on 31 July.

When he returned to track action with Poole, he wasn't the rider of old and found himself struggling. This led to thoughts of retirement at the close of the term, which had yielded 153 points from 24 league matches. However, during the winter he had a rethink and, after being transferred to St Austell, he recovered much of his sparkle to tally 135 league points – exactly the same total as his brother and fellow Gull, Ken! Ticker remained with the Cornish outfit in 1952 but suffered another loss of form and retired after scoring just 20 points in the Southern League (formerly Division Three).

Born: 25 June 1929, Forest Gate, London

Competition	Matches	Points
League	233	1,019½
National Trophy	43	232
Others	72	305
Three- and four-team tournaments	4	13
Pirates total	**352**	**1,569½**

Allan Kidd was a one-club man, riding only for Poole throughout his speedway days. He first practised at the *Speedway World* training school at High Beech, and if he had become disillusioned almost immediately nobody would have blamed him. The stories surrounding the start of his career tell of a lad who spent almost his last penny on a brand new machine only for the motor to blow up on its first outing at the King's Oak circuit! Undaunted, he fixed his machine, carried on training, and in a matter of weeks was showing sufficient promise to be able to go for trials at Poole. It had been hard work, but the youngster's steely determination to succeed had impressed the promoters at Wimborne Road, and he was duly signed on. All this happened in 1950, and on 31 May he proudly wore the Skull and Crossbones racejacket for the first time, scoring 2 points in a Third Division match at Tamworth as the Pirates claimed a 45-38 success.

After this promising debut, it was back to second-half races because competition for places was keen. However, he returned to the side for a home league match against Swindon on 19 June, netting 4 points in a 51-33 victory. By and large, Kidd was only called upon when someone else was injured, and by the end of the term he had ridden in 13 league matches, recording a total of 32 points. That tally included a season's best of 6 points when Poole defeated visiting St Austell 56-28 on 7 August. The Pirates ended the season as runners-up to Oxford in the Championship chase and the Londoner looked forward to more opportunities in 1951.

A lively close season ensued, during which Len Matchan and Geoffrey Bravery took over as the promoters, but happily for Allan he was retained by the incoming bosses. He was in the team right from the off and an early highlight was a contribution of 6+1 points when the Pirates beat near neighbours Southampton 45-39 in the Hants and Dorset Cup at Wimborne Road on 21 May. Unfortunately, the win was not without cost, as influential skipper Ken Middleditch suffered injury in a heat 14 spill. Shortly afterwards, as a result of this, Kidd found himself programmed at number one when Poole entertained Coventry in a challenge match on 4 June, and against opposition from a higher league (Division Two), he rose to the occasion to score a magnificent 10+1 points. Indeed, he only missed out on a maximum when beaten by Les Hewitt in heat 5. In what was a glorious campaign, the Pirates went on to land the Third Division Championship and Allan held his team place on merit throughout. In fact, he remained ever-present over the course of the 36-match league programme and accumulated 157 points for a very healthy 7.47 average.

With Poole gaining promotion to the Second Division in 1952, many pundits felt Kidd might benefit from spending a further season in Division Three, on loan to another club.

Nothing was further from his thoughts, or indeed the management's, however, and he was to stay on board the 'Pirate Ship'. Although he often rode at reserve, he was a reliable member of the side, and a final league tally of 133 points from a full quota of 44 matches yielded a remarkable 6.44 average. Poole were again crowned League Champions and Allan could look back with great satisfaction, especially given his limited experience. There can be little doubt that his best showing of the campaign occurred at home on 25 August, when he bagged 10 points in a 55-29 league success over long-distance travellers Ashfield (Glasgow).

In 1953 the Pirates ended the season in second position, behind Coventry, and for a third successive year Kidd remained ever-present over a reduced 32-match league programme to register 122 points. A high point was being selected to ride for Great Britain against the Overseas at Poole on 13 July, and he celebrated by scoring 3 points in a 59-49 victory.

It was very much the usual mix for the Pirates in 1954, with the side always amongst the league leaders throughout the campaign. In the end they were beaten to the title by a Bristol side that had dropped down after a difficult time in the First Division. With very little change to the Poole line-up, Allan again held his place for the duration, riding in 20 league matches for a valuable total of 99 points. The Skull and Crossbones were back to winning ways in 1955, taking the Division Two Championship at a canter from Coventry. The lad from Forest Gate really sparkled too, plundering 221 league points from 31 matches. Indeed, he missed just one fixture at Ipswich on 8 September, and that brought to an end an amazing sequence of 157 consecutive league appearances stretching all the way back to the last match of the 1950 season!

Having won the title, the question was, what next? Poole had remained in Division Two since their promotion in 1952 and the obvious answer was to step up to the top sphere of league speedway. This had been requested in the past and turned down flat; however, things were different in 1956, and the Pirates made their bow in the First Division. As had happened before, there were some who doubted the wisdom of Kidd stepping up, since it was

felt he might find the higher standard difficult to adjust to. Despite a number of team changes, he did hold on to his place though, and was far from disgraced in scoring 71 points from 22 league matches for a 4.79 average. He did his level best and had Poole stayed in Division One there is no doubt he would have done much, much better. As is well documented, however, Poole closed down, and Allan saw a future for himself and his wife in Canada.

The history books tell us that Poole reopened on an open licence later in 1957, prior to Vic Gooden moving his Rayleigh operation to Wimborne Road for 1958 and 1959. Then, in 1960, British speedway enjoyed its biggest move forward in years, with the formation of the Provincial League. Charles Knott took over the lease at Poole, made many improvements and entered the Pirates in the new league. He looked around for riders and, remembering Allan Kidd, offered him the team captaincy.

The first meeting at the revamped raceway was a World Championship qualifying round on 15 June, when the new skipper showed much of his old dash to accrue 12 points. His experience held the Pirates together in the early matches and, when the side was bolstered by Ken Middleditch, and later on Tony Lewis, he played his part in a late surge which only just saw them miss out on the Championship to Rayleigh. Looking at the statistics, he finished fourth in the club's scoring stakes, his tally of 104 points coming from 17 league matches. It was around this time that he also became something of a television star, appearing in an often-shown advert for Players Weights cigarettes. As well as featuring him in action on the track, the commercial also showed him at home with his wife.

In 1961 he found it a tad difficult to find top form, but such was the overall strength of the Pirates that they just powered to the league title. Appearing in 18 league matches, his contribution to another Poole success story was 80½ points, and he was as eager as ever for the 1962 season to arrive. Regrettably, he suffered a bad back injury at work, which was to spell the end of his career, whereupon he again emigrated to Canada. He has returned to see old friends on a number of occasions, and is always a more than welcome visitor at Poole Speedway, where 'loyalty' was always his middle name.

Born: 11 December 1958, Cambridge,

Competition	Matches	Points
League	26	300
Knock-Out Cup	2	25
Others	36	339
Pirates total	**64**	**664**

Michael Andrew Lee was the son of noteworthy European scrambles rider Andy, and was one of the few British riders of whom it is fair to say was born with an abundance of natural speedway talent. Co-author Glynn Shailes well remembers a meeting at Oxford in 1974 when the young Michael took part in a series of schoolboy exhibition races against Steve Naylor. The lad from Cambridge was simply sensational too, doing things on a speedway machine that riders much older would have been proud of. It was therefore no surprise when, in 1975, he received rave notices as a member of the Boston side in the New National League.

Amazingly, in his first season in the sport he thundered to 333 points from 37 league matches to average 9.13, recording no less than 10 maximums along the way (8 full and 2 paid). It was little wonder that British League King's Lynn also utilised his services as much as possible in an early form of 'doubling-up', and he never failed to impress, netting 165 points for a remarkable top-flight average of 7.53. His sensational form was recognised internationally when he received 3 Test caps for England against Australasia at Division Two level, and in the New National League Riders' Championship at Wimbledon on 27 September he scored 10 points and only just missed out on a podium position in a run-off.

After such a successful year, Lee moved up to ride on a full-time basis with King's Lynn in 1976, thereby gaining the opportunity to pit his skills against the best of the British League week in, week out. It didn't take him long to prove he was equal to the task either, as he chased hard after the popular Terry Betts for the position of the club's number one rider. The end of the term figures showed Betts had posted a league average of 9.66, while with 326

points from 34 matches, Michael's figure was 9.22. Capping a fine year, he raced to victory ahead of Steve Weatherley and Colin Richardson in the Junior Championship of the British Isles at Canterbury on 25 September.

In 1977, Lee was not only out on his own as the main man at King's Lynn, but his final average of 10.64 was also sufficient to put him at the very top of the entire British League averages, his nearest challengers being Ivan Mauger (10.62) and Peter Collins (10.49). The first of many full England caps came his way, with 5 Test appearances against the Rest of the World, while on the individual front, a marvellous World Final debut saw him card 12 points at Gothenburg on 2 September and only just miss out on third place after losing a run-off to the 'Great Dane' Ole Olsen.

Remaining at the head of the King's Lynn scoring, he plundered 375 league points to average 10.39 in 1978, while also continuing to add to his caps for England. A second World Final appearance at Wembley ended with a 9-point tally, his rostrum chances

severely dented by a last-place finish in his fifth outing.

At the end of the campaign, the ever-loyal Terry Betts left the Stars and was replaced by Dave Jessup, thus giving Michael stiff competition to retain his mantle as the club's top man in 1979. This he did, however, as 310 points produced a league average of 10.29, with Jessup not far behind on 9.80. The World Final was held at Poland's Slaski Stadium on 2 September and while Ivan Mauger was busy collecting his record-breaking sixth title, Lee accrued a tally of 11 points and then, in a run-off, defeated Kelly Moran, Billy Sanders and Ole Olsen to finish third overall.

In 1980, the diminutive Dave Jessup actually out-scored Michael for King's Lynn, ending the campaign with a league average of 10.52, compared with the 10.17 figure of his 'tall-in-the-saddle' colleague. Prior to that, on 5 September, the duo performed heroically in the World Final at the Ullevi Stadium in Gothenburg, Lee scoring 14 points to take victory while Jessup tallied a dozen and then defeated Billy Sanders in a run-off to secure second position. It was a night when the

British Lion well and truly roared, and one which has been talked about on many occasions since.

'Mike the Bike' was to stay with King's Lynn for a further two years, during which time he continued to score heavily, posting league averages of 10.34 and 9.47 in 1981 and 1982 respectively. He also made his fifth World Final appearance at Wembley on 5 September 1981, but on the night he enjoyed little luck and recorded just 5 points. He did have better fortune in the World Long-track Championship Final at Radgona, Yugoslavia on 20 September that year, however, when he rode brilliantly to take the title ahead of Christoph Betzl.

Despite his consistent high scoring, these last two years for the Stars were beset with problems for Lee, and he opted for a change of scenery which saw him move to the South Coast with Poole in 1983. Although the Pirates did not enjoy the best of seasons, the lanky lad from Cambridge just kept on piling up the points to finish with a league total of exactly 300 and an average of 10.43. So often he showed his class, but one match in particular typified the kind of performances the Poole fans had quickly become accustomed to. It was a home league encounter versus Coventry on 20 July and the Bees, led by Ole Olsen, raced to a 42-36 win. Michael, however, compiled a beautiful 12-point maximum and his pass of the quick-starting Olsen in the opening heat just had to be seen to be believed. It was timed to perfection, with the Danish maestro just not knowing where his opponent was coming from. The year also saw him make what was to be his last appearance in the World Final, and he bowed out of the sport's premier event with third place on the podium, courtesy of an 11-point total at Norden, West Germany, on 4 September.

Still with the Pirates in 1984, he began the season on song, but on 31 March, an incident occurred in a League Cup fixture at his former home, King's Lynn, which was to end in a ban. What happened was described in *Speedway Star* thus: 'Lee, who won the opening race at Saddlebow Road, was angered by the start of heat five, and after being left at the gate, rode along the track in the wrong direction, causing three other riders to take evasive action.'

He was fined by referee John Eglese and suspended from further participation in the meeting. The Speedway Control Board subsequently handed him a five-year ban for the events at King's Lynn, athough on appeal this was reduced to a year. It was, in effect, the end of his career as a Pirate, but in any case Poole's promoting company went into liquidation in January 1985, so no doubt he would have been on the move anyway. At the time of his ban, he hadn't ridden in a single British League fixture for the Pirates, although he had recorded 97 points from 11 League Cup matches.

Having served his ban, he made a comeback with King's Lynn in 1985, but problems just seemed to follow him around as he went about the business of mustering 90 points from 11 league meetings. Again with the Stars in 1986, he registered 114 points from 15 League Cup matches before the missing of a similar meeting at Sheffield on 12 June led to another fine and he was seemingly lost to the riding side of the sport.

In 1990, Michael announced that he wanted to return to the track, and after the outstanding fine from 1986 had been settled, he finally received permission to return with King's Lynn in 1991, having practised at length during the previous year. He started reasonably well, scoring 8+1 points at home to Oxford in a Gold Cup match on 23 March, but he had been away a long time and the going was tough. After completing 5 league matches for 17 points, he again seemed lost to the world of speedway. That was until a late-season bid to return with Poole ended with him suffering back injuries, following an engine blow-up whilst practising. That finally brought down the curtain on his career in the saddle – one that often left folk open-mouthed at his on-track capabilities. Indeed, fellow competitors often marvelled and asked, 'How did you do that?', and as so often with geniuses, he would simply reply, 'I dunno, I just did it'. Aside from numerous England caps, his career was littered with successes, the most notable being World Champion (1980); World Long-track Champion (1981); World Team Cup winner with England (1977 and 1980); and British Champion (1977 and 1978).

Born: 6 June 1923, Bournemouth, Dorset

Competition	Matches	Points
League	290	1,828
National Trophy & Knock-Out Cup	49	325
Challenge	111	753
Four-team tournaments	2	20
Pirates total	**452**	**2,926**

Anthony Edward Lewis claimed that he first saw speedway whilst on leave from the Navy in Australia. He was bitten by the cinder bug almost at once, but his enquiries regarding a trial Down Under came to nothing. Upon his return to these shores, it was to the grass-tracks of the south that he turned, meeting with some success. After three years on the grass, Tony thought he was ready for the cinder game, and after contacting the Poole promoters, he was offered trials. These proved successful and it wasn't long before he made his first appearance in the second half, riding in the Junior Scratch Race on 5 September 1949, after Poole had beaten Swindon 53-31 in a league match. He also got to ride in one full-blown meeting before the end of that year, when the Wimborne Road circuit played host to the Best Pairs Competition on 3 October. Yarmouth's Billy Bales had seized his motor whilst warming-up

before the start, and Lewis, as meeting reserve, was called upon to replace the unfortunate Bloaters representative, his contribution eventually being 2 points from 5 outings.

Having progressed well over a short period of time, he was ready to stake a claim for a team place in 1950, and his big opportunity arrived in a Third Division match at St Austell on 2 May, when he netted 3 points as Poole thundered to a 53-30 success. However, just a week prior to this, something rather special had happened, which was not only of great benefit to the club, but also helped the Bournemouth boy establish himself in the team. Ken Middleditch had joined the 'Pirate Ship', and Tony found himself partnered by the stylish former Hastings rider. The pair were to develop a wonderful understanding and their superb team-riding abilities became very well known in speedway circles. The locals in fact christened them 'Me and my Shadow', and their combined efforts were to realise many points for the cause of Poole. Lewis became a white-line rider of merit, and with Middleditch riding a mid-track course, the duo made sure the opposition just couldn't pass. Many years later, at a luncheon in Bournemouth, Tony talked with Glynn Shailes and Chris Broadway about his style of riding, professing that only two opponents ever managed to force him off his favourite inside line around the Poole track: 'They were Hugh Geddes, when riding for Swindon, and the one and only Ove Fundin of Norwich.' Continuing, he recalled: 'When Ove did it, his front wheel was well and truly on the grass, but he did move me over. Then again, he moved every rider over as he stormed through, no matter who they were!' Having established himself in the side, Lewis settled down well, and apart from missing 3 fixtures in late June he was to hold his team position to accumulate a season's total of 147 points from 28 league matches. Highlights were 10-point tallies in home matches against St Austell, Swindon and Liverpool, and his sterling efforts were rewarded when he was presented with the Freshman's Tankard for the best overall performance by a first-year Pirate.

Naturally, he was retained for the 1951 season, when new promoters took over and determined to bring success to the club. Indeed, the Pirates carried all before them as they raced to the Division Three Championship. Tony certainly played his part in a glorious campaign, remaining ever-present throughout the 36 league matches to accrue 240 points and average a healthy 8.08 figure. During the year, he was capped at England 'C' level against New Zealand, Sweden and USA. Two of the internationals he appeared in were held at Poole, and the one against Sweden on 13 August was memorable because the match opened with a fine 5-1 featuring him and Ken Middleditch, which the Wimborne Road regulars absolutely loved of course. When the Americans visited Dorset on a wet 6 September, they showed their class to win 62-46, but with 14 points to his name, Lewis was head and shoulders above his England team-mates as he virtually fought a one-man rearguard action.

Having gained promotion, the 1952 season was another one to savour for the Pirates as they simply steamrollered their way to the Second Division title. They were often referred to as a 'wonder' team, such was their strength in depth, and it was the likes of Tony who provided the firepower. Over a long 44-match league programme he again had a 100 per cent attendance record, scoring 285 points for an average of 7.90.

In 1953, it was very nearly a repeat performance from the Pirates, since they displayed marvellous form and team spirit. However, they were just pipped to the Division Two Championship by Coventry, although as has been well chronicled, they would surely have scooped another title had Brian Crutcher not been transferred to Wembley in early May. Lewis put together another season of consistent scoring to accumulate 187 points from 31

league matches, as his brilliant partnership with Ken Middleditch went from strength to strength.

In 1954, Poole were again there or thereabouts when it came to the challenge for Division Two honours. For a second successive year, they eventually had to settle for the runner-up position, with Bristol landing the Championship following the granting of their request to be 'demoted' from the top flight. With the league run over a reduced number of fixtures, Tony was as steady as ever in registering a tally of 110 points.

He again played a key role in 1955, recording 140 league points as the Pirates got back to their dominant best and sailed to the Division Two title ahead of Coventry. Despite the success, it was a season that ended very badly for Lewis. Having collected the silverware, the Poole management accepted an offer to appear in a short tour abroad, racing in Denmark, Finland and Sweden. An enjoyable trip was marred at Stockholm on 20 October, when Tony was involved in a bad crash, sustaining a fractured skull. Such were his injuries that his wife of just eight months was quickly brought to his bedside, where he was very ill indeed. Showing the kind of courage he always demonstrated on the track, he somehow pulled through though, and after making a full recovery, he eventually returned to his off-track job in the building trade.

So to 1957, a year which had seen Poole close to speedway, only for Lewis' father-in-law, Jack Crutcher, to re-open the track in late summer for a series of open-licence meetings. Tony helped on the administration side and in his spare time continued to maintain and clean his speedway gear so that it was ready for action at any given time. Nobody ever really thought he would actually resume in the saddle, but when the Provincial League was formed in 1960, he was keen to give it a go. Understandably, he preferred to make his track comeback away from Wimborne Road, and when he was offered a second-half spin at Cradley Heath, he jumped at the opportunity. By chance, it was after a match against Poole on 23 July, and if he was apprehensive about just how he would fare, then he needn't have been. Two storming wins were posted in his old

Poole on 7 September, when he superbly constructed successive 12-point maximums.

The Pirates finished that year in second place, only losing out on the Championship to Rayleigh on race points difference, but they made no mistake in 1961, storming to the title ahead of Plymouth. Lewis enjoyed a terrific time of it too, racking up 189 points from 19 league matches and also setting a new track record at Wimborne Road of 71.0 seconds on 10 May. He subsequently clocked the exact same time on 7 June, and was then joined as equal track record holder by Plymouth's Jack Scott on 28 June.

Poole retained the league title in 1962, when another 163 points flowed from Tony's wheels, and he again lowered the track record along the way, being clocked at 70.4 seconds on 2 May. Lewis remained on board throughout 1963 and 1964, hitting respective totals of 161 and 102 points, but upon the birth of the British League in 1965 he went into semi-retirement. The understanding was that he would still help out when required, and indeed he was to make 5 league appearances in 1967, and a further 11 in 1968, before hanging up his leathers for good. He later came back to Poole in another capacity, filling the role of team manager from 1973 to 1979 following the retirement of Ron Hart. A fine club man, he was always proud of the fact that speedway was his hobby and throughout his career he always kept his job in the building trade. As he once told co-author Glynn Shailes, 'Even if I was late back home after a meeting, I was still up early for work!'

familiar fashion and Ron Hart, the Pirates team manager, moved quickly to sign him up. A Knock-Out Cup match at home to Rayleigh on 3 August marked his return in a Skull and Crossbones race-jacket, and he went on to make 6 league appearances for a total of 60 points. Proving he was well and truly back, those half-dozen matches included a double-header against both Sheffield and Liverpool at

Born: 4 June 1944, Visby, Gotland, Sweden

Competition	Matches	Points
League	43	406
Knock-Out Cup	6	47
Others	13	100
Pirates total	**62**	**553**

Christer Lofqvist came from speedway stock, since his father, Fritz, had been a rider. Aside from his interest in the shale sport, Christer proved to be a bit of an all-round sportsman, also participating in football and ice hockey among other disciplines. Diminutive in stature, he initially took to the track in 1965, but his mother put an end to his racing ambitions, fearing that history might repeat itself – his father had died in an earlier track crash. Christer stayed away from the speedway scene for a couple of years, but upon his return to active racing he revealed his natural ability by winning the Swedish Junior Championship in 1967.

Recommended by Olle Nygren, he was subsequently signed by West Ham in 1970 and netted 7 points when making his debut in a home Division One match against arch London rivals Wimbledon on 12 May. His fearless style was well suited to the sweeping bends of the 415-yard Custom House circuit, and he went on to appear in 27 league matches, scoring 204 points for a healthy 7.82 average. Lofqvist had already been capped for his country in 1967, when he rode in 2 matches against Poland, and there were another 6 appearances for Sweden in 1970, versus Great Britain.

Back with the Hammers in 1971, he just pipped Swedish team-mate Olle Nygren for top spot in the team's league averages, posting an 8.75 figure, having accumulated 315 points from 33 matches. The year also saw him ride in one match for his country against England, as well as making his bow in the British League Riders' Championship at Belle Vue on 16 October, when he registered 8 points. Sadly, with Custom House Stadium being sold for housing development, West Ham withdrew from the First Division after the 1971 campaign, but this did mean that Christer was

to be identified down in Dorset as a member of the Poole side in 1972. His first meeting in a Skull and Crossbones race bib duly took place at Wimborne Road on 31 March, when he tallied 7+1 points in a 52-26 victory over Exeter in an Easter Trophy encounter. The Poole circuit was vastly different to the one he had become accustomed to at West Ham, but the exciting Swede simply took it in his stride and rode in the same all-out fashion. A week later, he found himself in action against his fellow countrymen, when the Pirates entertained Swedish touring team Vargarna. The home boys won a thriller of a meeting 41-37, with the track battles between Christer and his opponents Bengt Jansson and Hasse Holmqvist literally worth travelling miles to witness. Poole's new boy won just a single heat, when defeating former colleague Olle Nygren in heat 10, and had to give best to both Jansson and Holmqvist, although only after terrific scraps. Needless to say, he quickly became a hit with the generous Poole supporters, who have always taken to a trier, which Lofqvist most certainly was.

The league programme began at Swindon on 8 April, when the Pirates suffered a 50-28 pasting. However, the Swede scored 12 of his side's points and really made the home top two of Barry Briggs and Martin Ashby work hard for the maximums they recorded on the night. As the season progressed, there were more Test caps for Christer, plus selection for Sweden in the World Team Cup, and he also became the first Poole rider to qualify for the World Final proper since Brian Crutcher in 1952. The prestigious event was staged at Wembley on 16 September, and in a marvellous performance he plundered 11 points to finish in fourth position. Later, he represented Poole in the British League Riders' Championship at Belle Vue on 21 October, and in a meeting won by Wolverhampton's Ole Olsen, he recorded 7 points. At the end of the season it was good to see Lofqvist at the head of the Poole averages with a figure of exactly 9.00. He'd provided plenty of thrills and garnered 242 points from 27 league matches for a highly satisfactory first term in the Pirates' colours.

Staying with the Dorseteers in 1973, he rode even better, although his appearances were curtailed by commitments in his homeland and an ankle injury, suffered at Stockholm in September, which brought his season to a premature end. In fact, he only appeared in 16 league matches, but with 164 points and a massive 9.89 average, he was comfortably Poole's top man for a second successive year. Regrettably, Christer was never to turn a wheel again for the Pirates. In 1974, the BSPA banned commuting Swedish riders, so he, along with his compatriots, many of whom were established heat-leaders, had to remain at home in their native country. Despite this, he still made it through to his second World Final,

staged, somewhat ironically, at the Ullevi Stadium, Gothenburg, on 6 September, when he scored 8 points.

The British ruling didn't last for long, and in 1975 the Swedes were back in force. However, Poole had signed Malcolm Simmons, so Lofqvist was posted to Hackney, where he replaced the Oxford-bound Norwegian Dag Lovaas. Unfortunately though, he never really settled at Waterden Road and left the club after just 12 league matches, from which he took 84 points and averaged 7.61. He returned to Sweden, and that was that as far as his career in British speedway was concerned – he was allocated to Wimbledon in 1976 but never appeared, having been unable to agree terms with the Dons' promotion. It wasn't that long after, in February 1978, that the speedway world was saddened to hear that Christer had passed away due to the effects of a brain tumour.

Co-author Glynn Shailes fondly remembers an amusing story about one of the most spectacular Pirates of all-time, which centres around a meeting between Coventry and Poole. After leaving the gate, Christer rode high on the Brandon banking and drew level with his opponents and his team-mate. A Coventry fan, in his black and yellow garb, turned to a visiting Pirates supporter and remarked, 'He [Christer] will learn that you don't do that at Coventry – sorry mate.' Almost immediately, Lofqvist swooped down from the second bend and passed everyone on the back straight, to lead into the Binley Woods turn. 'I know,' replied the delighted Poole fan, 'but you see, no one's told him you don't do it!' Some years later, in 1989, his son Dennis came over to ride for King's Lynn, and during a four-year stint with the Stars he proved to be a steady scorer, although he was not the spectacular rider his father had been.

Born: 12 January 1971, Mtarfa, Malta

Competition	Matches	Points
League	51	617
Knock-Out Cup	11	107
Others	30	356
Three-team tournaments	2	19
Pirates total	**94**	**1,099**

Hailing from Malta as a consequence of his father being in the Army, Mark Royston Gregory Loram showed an early interest in schoolboy kart-racing, prior to graduating onto the grass-track scene. Having shown bags of natural ability, it wasn't surprising that he turned to speedway, taking his first such rides at Iwade when aged just nine. The youngster continued to hone his skills as the years passed, and in 1987 was offered a team berth with Hackney, duly making his debut for the Kestrels in a home challenge match against King's Lynn on 20 March. At the time, the London side had boldly opted to race in the British League, and although the going was hard, Mark never threw in the towel, ending the campaign with a commendable 5.52 average from 22 matches. Hackney reverted to the National League in 1988 and the move worked a treat as they swept all before them to lift the Championship in grand style ahead of Poole. Loram's contribution was immense: he chalked up 323 points from 26 matches for an average of 10.34, placing him second in the entire National League standings, just behind Poole's Steve Schofield (10.37).

Several bookings from the top-flight clubs came Mark's way during the year, and he also had an outing for Poole, totalling 9 points in a challenge match versus an Australian Select side at Wimborne Road on 31 May. He resisted the temptation to move up in 1989, instead accompanying the Hackney bosses in their transfer of National League operations to Ipswich. He was to enjoy a successful campaign with the Witches too, recording 373 points for a 9.68 league average, and capped the season by winning the National League Riders' Championship at Coventry on 9 September.

The lure of the British League was too great to resist in 1990 and it was to King's Lynn that he moved, his daredevil 'from-the-back' racing quickly becoming a feature of meetings at Saddlebow Road. Over the course of the season, he thrilled the Stars supporters time and again while accumulating 294 league points for a 7.85 average. In all, Loram was to spend five years with the Norfolk side, during which he was a sound scorer and entertainer supreme.

With 400 points and a league average of 9.42 to his name, the 1994 season was not only his last term in their colours, but also his best. The year also saw him make his World Final bow, and in a great showing at Vojens, Denmark, on 20 August he recorded 9 points in a meeting won by Swedish ace Tony Rickardsson.

A 21-team Premier League was formed in 1995, and having linked with Exeter, Mark was to enjoy two fine years as a Falcon, yielding averages of 9.82 and 9.36 respectively. He was also a mainstay of the Grand Prix during his time with the Devon side, netting 77 points in 1995 and a tally of 58 in 1996. There was a further change to the set-up of British speedway in 1997, when the Elite League came into existence, and with parent club Exeter opting to remain in the reduced Premier League, the Maltese-born racer joined Bradford on loan.

In a terrific year for the Dukes, they powered to the inaugural League Championship, with 'Loramski' playing a full part in the triumph by scoring 410 points and averaging 9.73. Aside from that, he was crowned British Champion at Coventry on 1 June, after defeating Chris Louis in a title run-off, both having tallied 14 points. Meanwhile, in the World Championship, he totalled 81 points from the Grand Prix series, with the undoubted highlight being a deserved victory in the final round at Vojens, Denmark, on 20 September, when he raced home ahead of Tony Rickardsson, Greg Hancock and Tomasz Gollob.

Despite Bradford's title success, the West Yorkshire club closed down, and although it was reported that Mark engaged in detailed talks with the Poole promoters, he ended up spending the 1998 season with Wolverhampton, for whom he registered an 8.34 league figure. Again a fixture of the Grand Prix, he slipped down the pecking order a little to finish the six-round series with 52 points.

After his year in the West Midlands, the streets of Dorset were buzzing with the news that Mark Loram would be joining the Pirates in 1999, and what a glorious year it turned out to be for him. In garnering 220 points from the short league programme of 18 matches, he averaged 9.91 and helped Poole to second place in the final table, just a point behind Champions Peterborough. However, on the world stage, things went even better. With 14 points, a second British Championship came his way at Coventry on 23 May, and his consistent riding was recognised when he earned a wildcard call-up for the Swedish Grand Prix at Linkoping on 4 June. In a marvellous performance he made it all the way through to the final, and then took victory ahead of Jimmy Nilsen, Tony Rickardsson and Leigh Adams. Deservedly, he retained his place for the remainder of the series, and whilst another GP victory eluded him, quietly and efficiently he went on to compile a total of 71 points.

In the series from the start in 2000, Loram didn't win a single round, yet his record was so good that he scooped the World Championship. Over the six-round series he made it to the final three times, and appeared in the consolation final on the other three occasions. His solidity throughout gave him a total of 102 points as he took the coveted crown from nearest challengers Billy Hamill (95), Tony Rickardsson (94) and Jason Crump (88). Needless to say, the Poole public were on cloud nine and afforded the sport's twenty-ninth World Champion a hearty reception upon his return to Wimborne Road. While he was competing with distinction on the individual front, domestically Mark continued to pile-up the high scores for Poole, ending the term with a 9.93 average, having netted 371 points from 30 league matches.

Unfortunately, the mega-popular rider and the Poole management were unable to strike a deal for the 2001 season, with the result that he went to Peterborough. He stayed with the Panthers for just one year, during which time he recorded an Elite League average of 8.36 and collected a third British Championship at Coventry on 26 May. A move back to the South Coast then saw Loram identified with Eastbourne in 2002, and he helped the Eagles to top the league, but in a dramatic end to the campaign it was Wolverhampton who took the title by defeating the East Sussex side in the final of the newly introduced Play-Offs.

Mark posted a league average of 9.51 that year, but in an injury-ravaged 2003, again with Eastbourne, he suffered a broken arm in April and a dislocated ankle in July, and his figure understandably fell back to 7.86. After grittily hauling himself back into the saddle following the two injuries, he finished the season well, and even made 3 guest appearances for Poole in the Knock-Out Cup, including both legs of the final, which saw the Pirates gain a 90-88 aggregate success over Coventry.

Following the introduction of a rider grading system, he joined Arena-Essex for the 2004 season, as the Purfleet side moved into the higher echelons of the Elite League for the first time. Capped many times by England over the years, Loram has continued to be a Grand Prix regular to the present day, although he has been unable to repeat the glory of 2000.

Born: 5 October 1925, Camberley, Surrey

Competition	Matches	Points
League	256	2,431½
National Trophy	47	575
Others	77	760
Three- and four-team tournaments	5	45
Pirates total	**385**	**3,811½**

Kenneth Arthur Middleditch began riding whilst serving in Egypt with the RAF. Having returned home, he determined to make a career out of the sport and during the winter of 1947 began attending a training school at Eastbourne. His progress was a little slow initially, but he then came on in leaps and bounds to secure a contract with Hastings in 1948. Like most promising novices Ken began with second-half outings, but such was his development that by July he was holding down a place in the Saxons side. In later seasons, particularly at Poole, he was to make his name as a team-rider and in that first year with Hastings he learned the art, riding with both Jock Grierson and Odsal loanee Bill Osborne. The end-of-term Division Three league table showed the Sussex side occupying a mid-table sixth position, with Ken's contribution to the cause being an excellent 166 points.

He went from strength to strength in 1949, however, blasting right to the top of the team's scoring with 393 points and there was many a promoter casting an eye on his talents. One such was former Bristol boss Reg Witcomb, who had moved on to Swindon and was busy trying to establish the cinder sport in the leafy Wiltshire town with a series of challenge matches. Witcomb had seen Middleditch in action at the new Blunsdon raceway on 20 August, when he stylishly raced to an 11-point tally for Hastings, helping his side to a 49-35 victory in the process. Just two weeks later, on 3 September, Swindon met Tamworth and Ken was booked in as a guest for the Robins. This time he recorded a magnificent 12-point maximum from a Swindon total of only 29. Meanwhile, with 54 points, Tamworth had

meted out a real hiding, but the man from Camberley stood alone as the star of the evening, having defeated all their heat-leaders in turn. At the end of the 1949 campaign, Hastings were forced to close after local residents had complained about the levels of noise. It meant Middleditch was available for transfer, but before any decisions could be made about his future in this country, he went off to ride in South Africa, where he performed with distinction.

Upon his return to the UK there was quite a scramble for his services, with Swindon believing they had got their man. However, like a number of other clubs, they proved unsuccessful with their bid, thought to be of £800, as he signed for Poole. Thus began a 'love affair' which was to see several honours come the Pirates way, with Ken excelling as a rider and later as team skipper. His club debut occurred in a Third Division fixture at home to St Austell on 24 April 1950, when he netted 6 points in a 50-33 win. Poole had endured a bit of a rough time in the early weeks of the

ing young rider by the name of Tony Lewis and the duo were to develop a magnificent team-riding partnership which had to be seen to be believed. The Poole faithful christened them 'Me and my Shadow' and quite rightly too. The pair were selected to ride for England 'C' in a Test match against Sweden at Poole on 13 August and they began the scoring with their customary 5-1, both finishing in front of the speedy Olle Nygren. To emphasise the magnitude of that feat, Nygren was to establish a new track record later in the meeting, clocking 70.0 seconds dead.

The Pirates remained unbeaten at home throughout the league programme, and indeed such was their strength that they only suffered 6 defeats on their travels. They claimed the Championship by 4 points from nearest rivals Exeter, being rewarded with promotion to the Second Division. Ken totalled 336 points from the 34 league matches he appeared in and his massive 10.47 average saw him perched nicely at the head of the club's figures. He then showed that he really was the leading player in his sphere of racing by going two places better than in 1950 to take the Division Three Riders' Championship at Cardiff on 23 October.

Having moved up a notch, Poole continued in the same vein in 1952, when the sensational Brian Crutcher became a fully blown heat-leader and took over as the team's most prolific points compiler. Ken wasn't far behind though, still scoring heavily (342 points from 40 league matches) and inspiring his side to great things. In fact, such was the power of the Pirates that they stormed to the Division Two title, winning it by 8 points from Coventry.

In 1953, despite having won their second successive Championship, Poole remained in Division Two: although they were always there or thereabouts, they ultimately finished in the runner-up spot, just a single point behind table-topping Coventry. The early transfer of Brian Crutcher to Wembley was clearly a contributory factor in this, for Poole would have almost certainly won the league had the 'Nipper' remained on board. With Crutcher gone, Middleditch once more assumed the mantle of the club's number one rider, scorching to 292 points in the league.

season, but the acquisition of Middleditch soon turned all that around, with the boys in blue and white becoming a real force as they chased after league leaders Oxford. In the end Poole had to settle for second place behind the Cheetahs, but Ken had enjoyed a fine time of it. He had accumulated 316 points from 32 league matches, captured the Wimborne Road track record and, for good measure, finished third in front of 23,000 spectators in the Division Three Riders' Championship at Walthamstow on 23 October.

In 1951, local businessmen Len Matchan and Geoffrey Bravery took over as promoters of the Pirates, and with Cyril Quick leaving to join Oxford, Middleditch got the nod as the new team captain. What an excellent appointment this turned out to be! During the previous season, he had been paired alongside a promis-

In a reduced Second Division programme, the 1954 season was almost a carbon copy of the previous one, as the Pirates again finished in second place. This was in no small way due to the fact that Bristol had asked to be 'demoted' from Division One after a difficult four-year stint in the top-flight. The Bulldogs were much more comfortable at the lower level and it was they who collected the Championship by a four-point margin. With 172½ league points, the consistent Ken remained the true leader of Poole, although he was chased hard by Bill Holden. Capping another fine year, Middleditch journeyed to Belle Vue for the Division Two Riders' Championship on 16 October and on a miserable wet night he showed his class to emerge triumphant.

The Camberley man spent a sixth term with the Dorset team in 1955, and in a glorious campaign he led them to the title, beating old rivals Coventry by 8 points. He headed the scoring with a massive 401 points but, having won the league again, the big question was: 'where do Poole go now?' They had moulded into a marvellous side and a number of the riders had been with the club since their Third Division days. The question was answered fairly quickly, however, when they found themselves promoted to the higher echelons of Division One. Ken had therefore skippered them through all three divisions of domestic racing and the team had earned promotion the proper way, by winning the league title.

The higher grade of racing came as something of a jolt and took some getting used to, with Poole finishing sixth out of the seven competing sides. Of all the team members who had risen from the Third Division, Middleditch was the most successful, recording 175 league points and finishing second to Jack Biggs (225) in the club's scoring stakes.

Supporters were rocked in 1957 when it was announced that Poole Speedway was to close due to a combination of petrol rationing and the unwanted expense of undertaking track alterations following instructions from the SCB. This resulted in a move to Swindon for Ken and he was to form a deadly partnership with Bob Roger, which played a major part in taking the Robins to the Championship. His contribution was 148 points from 19 league matches for an average of 7.54, with his team-mates including the likes of George White, Ian Williams, Neil Street, Ernie Lessiter and Mike Broadbanks. The world of business was calling, however, and at the close of the year, Middleditch called it a day at Blunsdon. He wasn't lost to the sport though, as Swindon sportingly agreed to him helping out back at Poole, who had reopened to league activity under the promotion of Vic Gooden in 1958. A freak happening in his first match back at Wimborne Road saw him hit a stray dog that had ventured on to the track, but he quickly overcame the shock to add another 72 points to his huge overall league tally for the Pirates. Although he retired at the end of the season, he made a comeback in 1960, when Charlie Knott Snr took out a lease on Poole Stadium and entered the Pirates in the new Provincial League. Ken finished the year behind Ross Gilbertson in the club's scoring, but with another 121 league points to his name he had played an important part in helping to re-establish the sport, with the boys in blue and white ultimately occupying second spot behind Champions Rayleigh, purely on race points difference.

A further season with the Skull and Crossbones followed and it was a year to savour as Poole thundered to another league title, finishing 7 points ahead of nearest challengers Plymouth. The remarkable Middleditch moved back to pole position on the Pirates scorechart, his league total for the year being 194 points. After that he did retire, although he made a single-match return to help a short-handed Poole against lowly visitors Bradford, scoring 10 points on 15 August 1962.

He was back again in 1966, but this time it was as team manager of the Pirates, and it was good to see him still serving the club he held so dear. This came about because the regular team boss, Ron Hart, took a year off, having been elected as Mayor of Poole. One of the club's finest servants, Ken enjoys his retirement at home in Sturminster Marshall and often pops along to Wimborne Road to view the racing. Although the track and stadium are different to when he performed so brilliantly, the place must hold a host of memories for him and all of them good.

Neil Middleditch

Born: 7 January 1957, Wimborne, Dorset

Competition	Matches	Points
League	313	1,513½
Knock-Out Cup	27	172
Others	152	738
Three- and four-team tournaments	19	128
Pirates total	**511**	**2,551½**

Neil Middleditch was the second son born to Poole legend Ken, who led the Pirates to much success in the 1950s, and was one of the sport's most loved and respected riders. It is worth recording that when Neil was born in 1957, Poole had actually closed down and his father ended up linking with Swindon for the season. The Wiltshire side had long admired Ken and his presence was to play a key part in the Robins' National League Championship success. That same year, Neil must have qualified as one of the youngest members of the Swindon Robins Junior Club, since the programme from a Blunsdon meeting on 25 May 1957 reported that two new recruits were Stephen Middleditch and his brother Neil, the latter at the time being less than five months old!

The young 'Middlo' was to follow the path of his famous father when he joined Eastbourne in 1973 and rode for the Dugard family, just as Ken had done way back in 1948 at Hastings. Prior to that, Neil had taken every opportunity he could to get rides, and one of the tracks he practised on was Reading's old base at Tilehurst. In those days, the home of the Racers had a ten o'clock shut-down, with the stadium lighting system run on a time clock which would see everything plunged into darkness on the stroke of the hour! Many's the time

Middleditch would be changed and ready to have a spin at the end of the second half, only for the clock to beat him.

As one can imagine, he was as keen as mustard to make good, and when he joined Eastbourne he found three ex-Poole riders in the Eagles squad in Ross Gilbertson, Mike Vernam and the evergreen Jimmy Squibb. However, through sheer ability he forced his way into the side and was to finish the season with a tally of 89 points from 22 Second Division fixtures for a 4.82 average.

Odd outings in the top flight also came his way, and these increased in 1974 while he continued to master his craft with the East Sussex outfit. Among others, he appeared in the blue and white of Poole, making his first appearance for the club in a home league match versus Exeter on 7 August, when he failed to score. He was to go on and ride in a further two Division One fixtures for the Pirates, netting 4 points at Exeter on 7 October and an impressive total of 6+1 against Belle Vue at Wimborne Road nine days later. There was little doubt Neil was on the threshold of great things and this was fully emphasised in 1975 when he pushed his Eastbourne average up to 9.62, having plundered 347 points in league racing alone. The Eagles finished fourth in the New National League but they went all the way in the Knock-Out Cup, winning the final against Workington, with Middlo hitting double figures in both legs. In what was a busy schedule, he also made 27 league appearances for Poole, yielding 84 points and an average of 4.43. Individual glory came his way too, when he won the Junior Championship of the British Isles after defeating Steve Weatherley in a title run-off at Canterbury on 28 June.

A full-time move to the 'Pirate Ship' beckoned in 1976, and he remained ever-present over the 36-match league programme to accrue 151 points for a creditable 5.01 average. He followed that up with an excellent year in 1977, during which he again rode in a full quota of league matches, increasing his average to 6.28 in the process. The highlight of a fine domestic campaign occurred on 28 September, when he produced a scintillating performance to record maximum points (12) in a 55-23 home victory over Bristol. During the season, Neil made it through to the British Final and also qualified for the European Under-21 Final, although he was subsequently banned from racing in the latter due to his progress in the World Championship!

The 1978 season turned out to be his best in a Skull and Crossbones race-jacket since, having scored 225 points, he posted a 7.65 league average. The tall-in-the-saddle rider was to stay loyal to the club until the end of 1984, during which time he took over the club captaincy (1980) and supplied a consistent level of points in the 'engine-room' department of the side. He was granted a much-deserved Testimonial in his last year with Poole and his big meeting, a four-team tournament, duly took place on 19 September, when an appreciative crowd paid tribute to a great servant.

The future of the Pirates looked bleak when the promotion, Poole Stadium Ltd, went into liquidation in January 1985, and the sport may possibly have been lost to the town had Weymouth bosses Mervyn Stewkesbury and Pete Ansell not subsequently transferred their operation to Wimborne Road to begin a new era for the club in the National League. Thankfully, Neil wasn't lost to the sport, as Arena-Essex paid a reported £5,000 fee to the BSPA for his services and he was a great success, finishing the year with a 9.49 league average. A season of both high scoring and huge enjoyment was crowned when he scooped the National League Riders' Championship with a 14-point tally at Coventry on 10 August. He stayed with the Hammers in 1986 but, despite posting a slightly increased league average of 9.65, he lost his position as the club's leading rider to the free-scoring Andrew Silver (10.52). Like his father before him, the business world then took over Middlo's life and although he continued to watch the action from the other side of the fence at Poole, that was it as far as active racing was concerned.

His love affair with the Dorset side continued, however, and in 1999, when Matt Ford and Mike Golding joined Pete Ansell as co-promoters, he was happy to accept the position of team manager. Later, in 2001, Neil took over the additional role of team boss of Great Britain, thus completing a full circle which had seen him capped for England during his riding career at full, Under-23 and National League level. In 2003, his great care at fostering team spirit paid dividends in the most spectacular fashion when the Pirates secured a glorious treble, winning the Elite League Championship, Knock-Out Cup and British League Cup. When the league title awards were handed out at the end of the campaign, an emotional Middleditch told the Sky Sports cameras of his love of Poole Speedway, proclaiming the occasion as the happiest day of his life. Indeed, it was a sentiment endorsed by all supporters of the Pirates. As far as club records are concerned, an overall total of 511 appearances sees Neil holding second place to Pete Smith in terms of the most meetings ridden for Poole. Come 2004 and Middlo is still enjoying life as manager of both Poole and Team Great Britain.

Born: 30 September 1935, Adelaide,
South Australia

Competition	Matches	Points
League	315	2,498½
National Trophy & Knock-Out Cup	22	241
Others	88	691
Four-team tournaments	5	51
Pirates total	**430**	**3,481½**

Before turning to speedway, Geoffrey Allen Mudge was a successful road racer and on one occasion actually finished as runner-up in the South Australian Grand Prix. His debut on shale occurred at Rowley Park, Adelaide, in 1958, and as if to emphasise just how capable he was as an all-round motorcyclist, he became Australian Long-track Champion the following year. Further proof of his abilities came later in his career, when he appeared in the World Ice Championships too!

In 1960, Geoff made his way to the UK to sign for Poole, who had joined the newly formed Provincial League, and there were also opportunities to ride in the second-half events at National League Southampton, since Charles Knott Snr was the promoter at both venues. Due to refurbishing at Wimborne Road, the Pirates made a late start to their home fixtures, so Mudge actually made his debut for the side in the first leg of the Vic

Gooden Trophy at Rayleigh on 22 April, when he tallied 4+1 points in a narrow 37-35 victory.

The Dorseteers initial league match took place three days later at the Stanley Stadium home of Liverpool, who were then also nicknamed Pirates, and Poole ran riot to win 47-25, with Geoff's contribution being a notable 7+3 points. The Wimborne Road raceway eventually hosted its opening meeting of the season on 15 June, with the staging of a World Championship qualifying round. The Aussie sported the number one race-jacket for the event and went on to record 8 points. His performance included an excellent race victory in heat 13, which gave rise to plenty of encouragement from the generous Poole crowd, the vast majority of whom were of course seeing him in action for the first time. The initial home league match was against Stoke on 29 June, and Mudge marked the occasion by scorching to a 12-point maximum in a 48-24 success. If there had been any lingering doubts about his ability, then that showing simply blew them all away and left everyone firmly believing the Pirates had a real winner on board. The boys in blue and white went on to make a determined bid for Provincial League honours, but in the event they were pipped at the post, on race points difference, by a strong Rayleigh outfit who, rather like the Pirates, had riders with bags of experience in their line-up.

Geoff enjoyed an excellent first campaign on these shores, netting 109 points from 17 league matches to finish third in the team's scoring, behind Ross Gilbertson (134) and Ken Middleditch (121). The record books also show that he registered a single league point for Southampton when called upon to assist the 'big sister' of Poole Speedway in a match against Swindon at Banister Court on 13 September. The Provincial League had proved to be a great success and its formation had given the British scene a real 'shot in the arm'.

Having just missed out on the title in its inaugural year of operation, Poole swept all before them as they raced to the Championship in 1961, finishing 7 points ahead of Plymouth. In Ken Middleditch, Tony Lewis and Ross Gilbertson, the Pirates boasted a powerhouse heat-leader attack, while Mudge provided the trio with very solid support. Indeed, he remained ever-present throughout the 20-match league programme to net a season's total of 139 points. Individually, he enjoyed victories at Rye House, in both the Whitsun Rose Bowl and the Gerry Hussey Memorial Trophy, thanks to 15-point maximums on each occasion. Meanwhile, at Eastbourne, he lifted the Hailsham Cup after defeating Roy Trigg in the final.

Not content with taking the league title in 1961, Poole went on to do it again in 1962, and it really was a year for Geoff to remember fondly. With Allan Kidd retiring, he was appointed skipper of the Pirates, and was to hold the post until 1970, after which he left for pastures new. He also took over as the club's top rider and led by example, registering 227 points from a full quota of 24 league matches. Adding to his list of achievements, he appeared for the Overseas in 5 Test matches against Britain, as well as carding a 9-point score in the Provincial League Riders' Championship, held at Belle Vue on 22 September.

Although Poole slipped down to third spot in 1963, there was more of the usual reliability from the Australian, whose record was a carbon copy of the previous year, with 227 league points being gleaned from 24 matches. The Pirates were part of the 'black' Provincial League in 1964, but the fans just continued to flock through the Wimborne Road turnstiles as normal, preferring to watch their favourites in track action rather than involve themselves with speedway politics. It turned out to be something of an indifferent season for both the team and Mudge, although being a true pro-

fessional he rode his way through the quieter patches and still ended up with 187 points to his name in league racing.

In 1965, it was 'kiss and make up' time between the National and Provincial Leagues, who came together to form the British League. This was the beginning of a new and exciting era for the sport in Britain, and Poole consolidated themselves in the new set-up, finishing tenth out of eighteen teams. Geoff was as solid as ever, riding in 28 league matches for 194 points and an average of 7.39. Under the Aussie's captaincy, the Pirates were to finish sixth in both of the following years, his contribution to the cause being 267½ points for a league average of 8.15 in 1966, and 286 points for an 8.19 figure in 1967.

The 1968 season was not one to savour for the ever-loyal supporters of the Dorset side, and with only 13 wins from 36 matches, their heroes slumped to seventeenth place in the re-titled British League Division One table. In spite of this, Mudge maintained his remarkable level of consistency, remaining ever-present to accumulate 278 points for a league average of 7.53.

Rather like good wine, he got better with age, and the 1969 season was to see him at his brilliant best, as Poole rose from the ashes to scoop the League Championship ahead of the mighty Belle Vue. Riding alongside Pete Smith, Odd Fossengen, Gordon Guasco, Bruce Cribb, Frank Shuter and Ted Laessing, he returned a 9.01 league average as the Pirates tracked a most solid septet. Indeed, when asked what their secret had been, the Poole skipper replied, 'Teamwork, and the determinaton to make up for the disappointments of the previous season.' On the individual front, a night that really stood out occurred at Poole on 21 May, when he plundered a 15-point maximum to win a World Championship qualifying round ahead of the sport's then reigning number one, Ivan Mauger.

The Pirates slipped to fifth spot in 1970, and it signalled Geoff's last term in the Skull and Crossbones race-jacket. He went out with another 282 league points to his name, but it still came as a major surprise when the man who had joined as a fresh-faced youngster in 1960 was granted a transfer to Reading. Really

he should have had a Testimonial for his service to Poole, but such things hadn't even been thought of in 1970, when he completed his eleventh successive season as a Pirate.

Upon linking with the Racers for their first season of Division One activity in 1971, Mudge was elected team captain, but he started the campaign with a problem, having fractured a kneecap in a grass-track meeting the previous October. This meant hospitalisation and a period out of the saddle, but he eventually returned to do a fine job, scoring 119 points from 19 league matches. Back for more in 1972, he thankfully avoided serious injury and represented the Berkshire side in 32 league matches, netting 188 points in the process. He then announced his retirement

and entered the business fraternity. However, it wasn't long before he made a return to speedway racing with Newport, partway through the 1973 season. He was to remain with the Welsh side until the end of 1974, but after failing to find his old form, he moved on to Exeter in 1975.

Geoff fared a little better with the Falcons, and finally called it a day after again riding in a few matches for the Devonians in 1976. He subsequently returned to his native land with his wife and family, but has visited the UK on a few occasions for holidays since. During his trips back to these shores, he never fails to call into Wimborne Road, the scene of many of his speedway triumphs, where he is justifiably afforded the warmest of welcomes.

Born: 2 July 1935, Falun, Sweden

Competition	Matches	Points
League	33	340
Knock-Out Cup	2	27
Others	10	100
Pirates total	45	467

Over the years Gote Nordin assisted several British clubs, usually on a 'helping out' basis since, due to the pressure of business, he was rarely able to devote himself to full-time speedway. If things had turned out differently and he had been able to race in the UK on a regular basis, it is likely he would have been crowned World Champion – he was certainly good enough. The nearest he came to winning the sport's major title came in 1961, the year the World Final moved from its spiritual home of Wembley Stadium to Malmo in his homeland. The Swedes swept the board to fill all three podium positions, with Ove Fundin being the victor ahead of Bjorn Knutsson, while Gote occupied third spot. Fundin dropped just one point on his way to glory and the man who showed him a clean pair of heels was Gote Nordin, in heat 19. Nordin still had a chance of finishing as runner-up overall, as he ended the meeting level on 12 points with Bjorn Knutsson and Barry Briggs. That necessitated a run-off, which saw Knutsson win at a canter, while Gote thwarted the ever-probing Briggs to ensure the Swedish one-two-three.

Prior to that, in 1960, the man from Falun found himself allocated to Belle Vue to begin his time in British racing, but with a number of Swedish commitments to fulfil he did miss a considerable number of National League fixtures. As it was, he netted 58 points for the Aces in league racing and had he been available more often the Manchester side could well have taken the title. Instead, that honour went to Wimbledon by a 3-point margin from Belle Vue.

Despite his obvious talent, the Aces were denied Nordin's services in 1961, and it was not until 1964 that he reappeared in the UK. With the National League down to just seven teams and Wimbledon suffering from a short-

age of heat-leaders, it was to the Dons he was posted. It was the opportunity for him to shine, and this he certainly did. He had clearly come on since his stint with Belle Vue, and he had added to his World Final appearances in the Wembley-staged events of 1962 and 1963, scoring 9 and 10 points respectively. Having qualified as second reserve in 1964, he did not get to ride on the night, but when the triumphant Barry Briggs returned from the big meeting in Gothenburg, Sweden, it was Gote who became the first rider to defeat the (then) three times World Champion. Wimbledon were the visitors to Swindon for a league match on 12 September and after Briggs had gone on a special parade in order to receive the cheers from his own supporters, Nordin thundered to a 12-point maximum, twice beating 'Briggo' in heats 1 and 6. The record books credit him with a season's tally of 137 league points for the Dons, and this figure was sufficient to make him the highest scorer in the entire league.

1965 saw the formation of the British League, and commuting foreigners, who were in the main Swedish, were barred from competing. They were, however, welcomed back in 1966, whereupon Gote signed-up for Newport.

Being a class act, he quickly settled on the Somerton Park raceway and became the master of it. Often, while his team-mates struggled for points, he simply got on with the job of clocking up high scores – week in, week out. The end-of-term statistics made impressive reading, for the Swede had ridden in 31 league matches and registered 352 points for a huge 10.53 average. So good were his figures that only two riders actually finished with higher averages in the British League, these being Swindon's Barry Briggs (11.08) and Coventry's Nigel Boocock (10.67). Nordin also qualified for the World Final at Gothenburg, but on a night when he was expected to do particularly well, a heat 13 fall didn't help his cause and he ended the meeting with 9 points. It's impossible to leave the 1966 season without reference to the magnificent performance of Gote in the star-studded Internationale at Wimbledon on 30 May. A brand new Jawa was the prize up for grabs and, cheered on by hordes of Welsh fans, he completed a wonderful 15-point maximum to win in style.

After such a successful term with Newport, the management of the Welsh outfit naturally wanted him to stay, but it was to Poole where 'Gentleman Gote' went. As could be expected, the Newport supporters weren't best pleased, but the request for a move came from the rider himself. He had seen something in the Wimborne Road circuit and obviously wished to be part of the Pirates' set up in 1967. Poole opened the season with a home Easter Trophy match against Exeter on 24 March, and although they suffered a shock 40-37 defeat, the speedy Swede was right in the groove, scoring a 12-point full-house. The return match at the County Ground on 27 March also resulted in defeat (49-29), although Nordin was quite superb in plundering 14 points, only missing out on another maximum when defeated by the lively Chris Blewett. The Poole fans knew they had a star on board and looked forward to regular top-drawer showings. In the main they got them too, but on the odd occasion when they didn't, the grapevine would immediately be buzzing with stories that Gote was ill, in dispute with the Poole management, suffering from jet-lag and a whole host of other reasons. All this was nonsense of course; the simple fact

was that he COULD be beaten – but not that often! Long Eaton travelled to Wimborne Road for a league match on 5 April and included in their side was a promising Swede, one Anders Michanek, who in heat 12 gained revenge for an earlier defeat to spoil Nordin's chance of a maximum.

Gote continued to score heavily for the Pirates and when Wimbledon staged the prestigious Internationale on 29 May, he produced a carbon-copy display of the previous year to win the all-star event with 15 points. In addition, he skippered Sweden to a 3-2 Test series victory over Great Britain, his best performance being a 17-point haul at Wimbledon in the first match on 15 June. The day before had seen Poole host a controversial Knock-Out Cup tie versus Halifax and, despite arguments over track conditions, Gote made light of the complaints by scoring the lot (15). The examples of his fine riding are endless and at the close of the campaign he had accrued 329 points from 32 matches for a league average of exactly 10.00.

The many Dorset fans looked forward to more of the same in 1968, and after racing in the Easter Trophy matches against Exeter, he constructed a paid maximum (11+1) versus Wimbledon at home in the Pirates' first league match of the season on 17 April. Regrettably, that was to be the sum total of his second year with Poole, since he then departed to concentrate on his business ventures. Thankfully though, Nordin wasn't completely lost to the British speedway scene. Despite the fact he wasn't able to ride on a full-time basis, he did enjoy spells with Coventry (1969), Wembley (1971) and Halifax (1972), and such was his ability that he always filled a heat-leader berth with ease.

Many years later, he made a nostalgic return to Poole for a Golden Greats meeting on 13 September 2000, when he demonstrated much of his old dash before mechanical problems affected his steed. The following year, on 25 July, he once more donned a Skull and Crossbones race-jacket, as a Poole Past & Present side entertained Briggo's World Select. Then sixty-six years of age, Gote did well too, his tally of 6 points including a race win, although his efforts were unable to prevent a 50-41 defeat for the Pirates.

Born: 10 March 1923, Camberwell, London

Competition	Matches	Points
League	92	614½
National Trophy	8	65
Others	9	72
Three- and four-team tournaments	2	6
Pirates total	**111**	**757½**

In a family connection with speedway, Frederick Pawson's brother, Ernie, rode for Crystal Palace prior to the Second World War, and was subsequently identified with Eastbourne in 1947, when the Eagles became founder members of the Third Division. Having served abroad with the RAF, it was after the hostilities that Fred himself, became interested in the sport, being kept busy as a mechanic, not only for his brother, but also for other members of the Eastbourne team. This involvement inspired him to try his luck on the track, and like many would-be riders had done before, he set off for training and practice at Rye House. Whilst undergoing his speedway 'apprenticeship', he came to the attention of the Harringay management, who duly signed him on. This was in the March of 1948, but it was clear that Fred needed to gain racing experience, so he found himself loaned out to Poole, who were busy team-building for entry to Division Three. The Pirates promoters had established a working relationship with the London outfit, and in addition to Fred, a couple of other Harringay juniors, Sid Clark and Joe Bowkis, were also to find themselves racing in Dorset.

Poole initially took to the track in a league match at Tamworth on 14 April, when Pawson was in the main body of the eight-man team. Unfortunately, the virgin side were no match for the home team, who handed out a real licking to win 63-21, with the Londoner netting 3 points from the number six berth. The Pirates subsequently raced for the first time on their home circuit at Wimborne Road on 26 April, when Great Yarmouth provided the opposition for a National Trophy tie. The match was marred by a very bad crash in the opening heat, which tragically resulted in visiting rider Reg Craven receiving injuries that were to prove fatal eight days later. Poole went on the win the meeting by a huge 74-32 scoreline, and in a fine home debut, Fred tallied 8+1 points from 5 starts.

As the season went on he was to make excellent strides, his efforts finally yielding a total of 231½ points as he remained ever-present over the 44-match league programme. Interestingly, the half-point occurred in a home match against Plymouth on 12 July when, with visitor Pete Lansdale winning by some distance from Sid Clark in heat 11, the ACU Steward just couldn't separate Pawson and Vic Gent as they flashed across the line together for third position. The highlight of his year, however, happened much closer to the end of the campaign, on 13 October, when he hit top form to net a glorious 12-point maximum as the Pirates went on the rampage to beat visiting Wombwell 58-26. Immediately prior to that, Pawson was a member of the Poole side that undertook a short tour of Sweden, his best performance being 10+2 points in a 45-27 success at Linkoping on 6 October.

In 1949, while both Joe Bowkis and Sid Clark returned to Harringay, Fred continued with the Dorseteers. It was to be a fine term for him too, and the points were to really pile up. It didn't take him long to strike top form either, and following scores of 10 points at Plymouth, and 11 at home to Great Yarmouth, he got 'the lot' (12) against visiting Hanley on 2 May. The match was a thriller, but even Pawson's brilliance couldn't save Poole from suffering a narrow 43-41 defeat. That was the beginning of a real golden spell for the Camberwell-born racer, since he followed it up with successive 12-point maximums at home to Halifax and away at Rayleigh. In fact, his run almost stretched to 4 full-houses in a row, but having registered 3 straight wins against Oxford at Wimborne Road on 16 May, he unluckily fell in his fourth outing when yards in front. Over the course of a marathon 48 league matches, he was again ever-present and a final total of 383 points represented tremendous progress from a rider who, after all, was only in his second year of racing. In fact, he finished just behind the club's leading scorer, Cyril Quick (386½), and was rewarded with a handsome trophy by the Supporters' Club. He had contributed greatly in the team-riding department, and his partnership with Dick Howard was a joy to watch.

It was clear that Fred, or 'Our Freddie' as he was known by thousands down Poole way, would be heading back to Harringay in 1950, but things didn't go as expected with the Racers. The London boys endured a difficult year, finishing 8 points adrift at the foot of the Division One table, with Pawson posting an average of 3.78 having accrued just 79 points

from the 30 league matches he appeared in. This wasn't a true reflection of his ability of course, but it was no real surprise when he was transferred to Second Division Norwich in 1951. Happily, his form returned, and with a season's total of 178 points, he helped the Stars to win the League Championship. During the year, he was invited down to Poole on 28 September, to take part in the second half of a Division Three meeting that had earlier seen the Pirates thrash St Austell 57-27. He thoroughly enjoyed being back among some of his former team-mates too, firstly beating Ken Middleditch in a special match race and then winning the Invitation Final ahead of Brian Crutcher, Terry Small and Roy Craighead.

In 1952, promoted Norwich found it tough going in the First Division and, not unexpectedly, ended up in the basement position. Fred had a better time of it than in his previous stint in the top tier, however, gleaning 150 points from a full quota of 36 league matches for an average of 5.06. Still with the Stars in 1953, his scoring dropped to 49 points from 15 Division One matches, and he subsequently disappeared from the domestic scene after scoring only 5 points from 3 matches in 1954. He had become accustomed to visiting New Zealand during the close-season breaks from domestic racing, and in fact during 1952/53 had ridden for England against the Kiwis at Wellington, registering a useful 6-point total. It therefore surprised no one when he made his permanent home in New Zealand, where he lives to this day.

Last year, word came through that Freddie had passed away, but this wasn't so, and in true Mark Twain style he was able to e-mail Britain with the news that 'reports of my death have been greatly exaggerated'. Always admired by the knowledgeable Poole supporters, he receives a great reception when, from time to time on his holidays, he returns to the scene of his best racing days.

Born: 15 July 1958, Newport Beach,
California, USA

Competition	Matches	Points
League	51	445
Knock-Out Cup	5	58
Others	28	194
Three- and four-team tournaments	5	42
Pirates total	**89**	**739**

Ronald Nunan Preston took his first speedway rides when aged sixteen, having initially been a keen moto-crosser. It was said that he actually sold his moto-cross bike in order to finance his speedway desire, and after switching disciplines he progressed steadily. In 1979, he made his way to the UK to sign for Poole, although in truth, few had heard of him when he lined up for the Pirates in their opening challenge match of the season against visiting Reading on 21 March. Despite trying very hard, there was to be no dream debut for the Californian and from 4 outings he scored just a single point as the Poole team crashed to a 45-33 defeat.

The Pirates raced at Wimbledon the following evening in a Gauntlet Gold Cup meeting and Ron fared a little better, netting 3 points. The match resulted in a 48-30 loss for the side from Dorset, but the promise of the American was evident to all at the plush Plough Lane venue. Grittily, he plugged away over the next few matches and 11 April was to prove a day to remember: Poole entertained Eastbourne in another Gauntlet Gold Cup fixture, and whilst the boys in blue and white suffered a 43-35 defeat, Preston covered himself in glory by topping the scorechart with a paid 12 points (9+3) from 5 starts. This was to be his highest home return in the Gold Cup competition, with 6 points being his best away tally at Exeter on 16 April. The Pirates were handed a real pasting, going down 54-24, but Ron gave everything around the vast County Ground bowl and was worth every one of his half-dozen points. Happily, he was finding his feet and adjusting to the pace of top-flight British racing. He emphasised this with a

score of 7+2 points when Poole entertained Leicester in their first league match of the campaign just two days later.

While he continued on a fast learning curve, it has to be remembered that he was seeing the away circuits for the first time. Undeterred, the American ace recorded 9 points in a cracker of a match at Hackney on 1 June, when the Pirates narrowly went down 41-37. Five days later, he produced a wonderful showing to secure a first paid maximum (11+1) in a 44-34 home victory over King's Lynn. The points kept coming thereafter, but the highlight of Preston's year undoubtedly occurred in Leningrad, Russia, on 22 July, when he appeared in the final of the European Junior Championship. After running a third-place finish in his opening ride, he reeled off four straight wins to total 13 points and take overall victory from Russian Airat Faljzulin. After his success, Ron delighted the Wimborne Road patrons with as good a full-house (12) as ever witnessed in a league match, against Ipswich on 8 August. Home maximums followed versus Hull (15) and Sheffield (12), before he completed his first British season in

style by posting an unbeaten 12-point tally at Birmingham on 1 October. From arriving on these shores as a virtual unknown, he had emerged as the find of the season, a fact borne out by a phenomenal home league average of 10.25 – a higher figure than that of club number one Malcolm Simmons. Overall, however, Preston scored 261 points from 30 league matches, and his impressive 8.71 average put him just behind the ever-reliable 'Simmo' (8.93) in the club's statistical run-down. It is impossible to leave the 1979 season without mentioning the Tommy Jansson Memorial Trophy at Wimbledon on 5 July, in which 'Rapid Ron' scored 14 points and finished as runner-up to Dons favourite Edward Jancarz after losing out to the Pole in a title run-off.

The lively Californian was back with the Pirates in 1980, when the faithful Skull and Crossbones supporters looked forward to plenty of sensational points-plundering from him. Unfortunately, he endured a troubled first half of the year, during which he firstly suffered a dislocated shoulder in a Gauntlet Gold Cup match at home to Eastbourne on 7 April. Then, on 14 May, he damaged a knee in a heat 9 crash whilst representing the USA in

the fourth Test match against England at Poole. The latter knock took its time in healing, but after missing numerous matches he returned with a paid maximum (9+3) in a home league encounter against Halifax on 23 July, and was to continue in the same free-scoring groove as witnessed the previous season. There was a maximum return (12) against a visiting Cradley Heath outfit on 13 August and he went on to total 184 league points for an increased 9.09 average. As touched upon, international caps came Preston's way in between his early-season injury problems, when he represented his country in 4 Test matches against England, his best performance being 8 points at Wimbledon on 1 May.

In 1981, he was again stationed at Poole for what should have been a great personal season, but it wasn't to be. A recurrence of his knee injury was serious enough for him to return to his homeland for surgery, this coming after he had shown good form in the League Cup to accumulate 98 points from 11 matches. Aside from that, he only appeared in one other match for the Pirates, scoring 12+1 points in a Knock-Out Cup tie at National League Mildenhall, as the boys in blue and white went on the rampage to triumph 58-38. He also rode in two more Test matches against England at Belle Vue and Poole, netting tallies of 3 and 6 points respectively.

Having recovered fitness, a change of track saw the mega-popular American link with Eastbourne in 1982, with a reputed fee of £10,500 being paid for the acquisition of his services. In what was to be his last term of British activity, he enjoyed a fine campaign to record 223 points from 22 matches, his 9.87 average putting him just outside the top ten in the entire British League. Having been made club captain, it was a huge blow to the Eagles when Ron didn't return in 1983, and there is no doubting how much he was missed, not only by the East Sussex side, but by shale-sport fans at large.

Born: 19 January 1919, Taunton, Somerset

Competition	Matches	Points
League	87	736½
National Trophy	6	60
Others	20	160
Three- and four-team tournaments	2	23
Pirates total	115	979½

West Country lad Cecil James Quick was known throughout his speedway career as Cyril. His racing days began on the grass-track circuits in 1937, and he met with some degree of success until joining the forces at the outbreak of war. He enjoyed his first taste of speedway at one of the Monday-night practice sessions at Bristol in 1946, and continued thereafter to train as a pupil at Tiger Stevenson's school. Quick proved a fast learner, and having been handed a team spot with the Bulldogs in 1947, he was to ride in every one of the club's 28 Second Division fixtures, carding exactly 100 points in the process. He again lined up for Bristol in 1948 but, as so often happens to riders in their second term, it was a case of simply 'standing still'. Cyril gleaned a total of just 69 points from 22 league matches, and it came as little surprise when, at the end of August, he requested a transfer away from the Bulldogs for 'personal reasons'.

Division Three side Great Yarmouth were interested in securing his services, but the Control Board refused to sanction the move, since the transfer deadline date had passed. He was subsequently allowed to join Poole though, and made his debut for the side in a Division Three encounter at Hull on 11 September, when he posted 7 points in a 47-36 reverse. The Control Board had apparently given 'special dispensation' for his move, since the Dorset outfit had suffered a number of injuries to key riders and needed strengthening as a matter of urgency. Quick subsequently made his home debut for the Pirates against Coventry two evenings later, when he raced to a brilliant 11 points in a 47-37 defeat, only missing out on a maximum when losing to visiting skipper Bob

Fletcher in his final ride. On 14 September, the Pirates visited Great Yarmouth for a league match, and although Cyril sped to an impressive 10-point tally, he was unable to prevent his team from losing 45-39.

Regrettably, his first period in Poole's colours was to be all too brief, as he then suffered a broken leg in a grass-track meeting, which rendered him out of action for the remainder of the season. He had worn the Skull and Crossbones race-jacket in just 3 league matches and recorded a total of 28 points. However, having returned to fitness, Quick was back with the Pirates in 1949, when he was not only made skipper of the team, but in a season that saw the Third Division programme run over a mammoth 48 matches, he remained ever-present to top the club's scoring with 386½ points. He always led the side by example and registered three 12-point maximums along the way, including one at Plymouth on 28 July when he also went on to win his heat and the final of the Pennycross Scratch Race in the second half. Prior to that, an individual highlight came at

97

Wimborne Road on 4 July, when with a faultless 15-point maximum he plundered the Lucky Stars Trophy ahead of a quality field.

The 1950 season began badly for Poole, with the team being somewhat weakened by Fred Pawson's recall to parent club Harringay. Cyril continued to score heavily for the Pirates, but it was clear he needed help, and this came in the form of a rider who was one of the very best in the league, namely Ken Middleditch. The former Hastings rider helped transform the Dorseteers into a formidable outfit, and they were eventually to finish as runners-up to Oxford in the Championship chase.

With fewer teams competing in the Third Division, Quick again appeared in every meeting of Poole's reduced 36-match programme, once more heading the scoring stakes with 322 points. During the year, the Lucky Stars Trophy was again held at Poole on 31 July and, showing that he wasn't prepared to relinquish the title, he reeled off another perfect 15-point tally. At the end of the season, scores of Poole fans made the journey to Walthamstow for the inaugural Division Three Riders' Championship on 23 October, but despite being one of the favourites for the prestigious event, Cyril came away with only 6 points to his name.

He was again expected to lead the Pirates in 1951, but it was not to be. Poole Speedway suffered a traumatic winter, with an eleventh-hour change of promotion seeing Len Matchan and Geoffrey Bravery taking over from Cliff Brewer. Prior to this, Quick had requested a transfer, and the new bosses were unable to persuade him to change his mind. A hefty fee subsequently changed hands and he linked with Oxford, who had been promoted to Division Two as a result

of their Championship success. However, for reasons that remained a mystery, he just could not settle with the Cheetahs in their early challenge matches and Southern Shield fixtures. Before he had ridden a single league match for them he was loaned out to Great Yarmouth (who were then also a Division Two side), for whom he registered 142 league points, and at least recovered some of his best form. In 1952, Poole co-promoter Len Matchan, became involved in the running of Southern League side Wolverhampton, and straight away, he began to strengthen what was a woefully weak team. One rider he immediately sought was Cyril Quick, who didn't hesitate in putting pen to paper. He enjoyed a great season too, accumulating 272½ points from league matches alone to finish above Benny King (266) at the head of the club's scoring. Having regained all his old sparkle, great things were expected from him in 1953, but instead, he made the decision to retire in order to concentrate on his business interests.

Perhaps one of the best races of his career took place at Swindon on 10 September 1949. The main meeting saw him captain a combined Swindon and Poole side in a challenge match against Liverpool, and the programme of events was also scheduled to include match races between Bill Kitchen, skipper of the famous Wembley Lions, and Bill Longley of New Cross. Unfortunately, Longley couldn't attend, so Cyril took his place, and to the joy of those present, he clocked a good time to beat Kitchen in the first race. Although the Wembley man had his revenge in the two following races, it had been a fine effort from the then Pirate, who went on to top-score with 11 points as his composite side defeated Liverpool 43-40.

Born: 17 August 1970, Avesta, Sweden

Competition	Matches	Points
League	90	1,104
Knock-Out Cup	12	144
Others	24	280
Three-team tournaments	3	23
Pirates total	129	1,551

Jan Tony Soren Rickardsson first sat on two-wheeled machinery at the age of just four, and seven years later he moved on to the junior speedway scene in his native Sweden. He continued to perfect his skills and subsequently made his first appearance in this country in 1988, when he toured with Getingarna under the managership of the former Newport thrill-maker-in-chief Torbjorn Harrysson. The Swedish side raced in challenge matches at Oxford, King's Lynn, Reading and Swindon, but it wasn't really a tour to remember for Tony since his best return was 3+2 points in the meeting at Blunsdon on 26 March. Former Oxford team manager John Tremblin had arranged accomodation for the team in a pleasant guesthouse at Wootton Bassett and also supplied workshop space so the lads could work on their bikes. Little did anyone in the quiet Wiltshire town realise that they were in the presence of a rider who would one day dominate the World Championship, taking the crown on no less than five occasions!

During 1990, Rickardsson gave notice of what was to come by battling through to the final of the World Junior Championship, staged at Lvov in the Soviet Union on 9 September. The meeting had a classy line-up and the Swede did well to net 10 points, before defeating Jaroslaw Olszewski in a run-off to give him third place behind winner Chris Louis and runner-up Rene Aas.

In 1991, he made an important decision about his speedway future when he decided to race in Britain full-time. He linked with Ipswich and duly made his club debut in an inter-league challenge match at Peterborough on 22 March. Showing just how much he had learned since that short British tour in 1988,

he recorded 3 wins on his way to a tally of 10+1 points and suitably impressed everyone who saw him that night at the East of England Showground. In an outstanding first season for the Witches, Tony went on to bag 208 points from 21 league matches for an average of 8.26. As well as riding well for the Suffolk club, he also graced his first World Final, held in his homeland at the Ullevi Stadium, Gothenburg, on 31 August. In a superlative display, he notched a dozen points to finish as runner-up to the pint-sized Dane, Jan O. Pedersen.

Remaining with Ipswich in 1992, Rickardsson accumulated 226 points and upped his Division One average to 8.42. Again, he qualified for the World Final, held at the Olympic Stadium in Wroclaw, Poland, but in a meeting won by future Poole team-mate Gary Havelock, he finished well down the field on 5 points.

A league average of 9.03 placed him inside the top ten First Division riders in 1993, when he again represented Ipswich. Somewhat surprisingly though, he was unable to reproduce his domestic form in the World Final at Pocking, Germany, where he mustered just 4 points. The season also saw him don a Poole race-jacket for the first time, when he guested in the opening league match of the season at Cradley Heath on 27 March, recording 6 points from 4 starts.

1994 was to be his major breakthrough year, with the staging of the last traditional-style World Final at Vojens, Denmark, on 20 August. In a wonderful showing, Tony compiled 12 points to end the meeting level with both Hans Nielsen and Craig Boyce prior to taking the title in a dramatic run-off after shooting past the faster-starting 'Main Dane' at the end of the first lap.

Rickardsson decided to take a break as far as British racing was concerned – after all, he had a very busy schedule in the Swedish, Danish and Polish leagues to concentrate on. However, while Ipswich sought a replacement, he did agree to help out at the start of the season, riding in a single league match and another in the Knock-Out Cup. It wasn't until 1997 that he made a return to the UK and during the interim he raced in the first two Grand Prix series, finishing second in 1995 and fourth in 1996.

Although it is perhaps not well known, as the 1997 season unfolded, Poole, who were enduring a difficult campaign, made enquiries about signing Tony, but it was to Ipswich he eventually returned in August. It was the inaugural year of the Elite League and the super Swede went on to appear in 11 such matches for a 10.04 average, finishing second only to Belle Vue's Billy Hamill (10.17) in the overall figures for the new domestic competition. On the World stage, Rickardsson again ended up with a fourth-place finish in the Grand Prix series, but in 1998, he was to go all the way and claim a second World Championship ahead of fellow countryman Jimmy Nilsen. Meanwhile, he helped Ipswich to a glorious treble triumph as they swept all before them to win the Elite League Championship, Knock-Out Cup and Craven Shield. Tony was head and shoulders above everyone else in the entire league, plundering 431½ points from 32 matches for a 10.29

average, and with Chris Louis (9.42) and Tomasz Gollob (9.29), formed a devastating attack for the Witches.

Following the club's wonderful achievements, there was a huge surprise when it was revealed that both co-promoter Mike Western and Rickardsson were on the move to near neighbours King's Lynn for the 1999 season. The Swede enjoyed another great campaign, posting a league average of 10.05 for the Knights, while further individual success came his way with a third World title.

He was again absent from British racing in 2000, a year when he had to settle for third spot in the Grand Prix series, behind Champion Mark Loram of Poole and Coventry's Billy Hamill. As things turned out, the Pirates' bosses were unable to agree terms with Loram for the 2001 season, but Matt Ford promised the fans they would find the best replacement possible. He was as good as his word too, since a deal was done to finally bring Tony Rickardsson on board the 'Pirate Ship'.

Double figure returns were the norm as his efforts, combined with those of Krzysztof Cegielski and Gary Havelock at the top end, helped Poole challenge for the Elite League Championship. In the end, Oxford pipped them by just a single point, with the Swede's contribution to the cause being 327 points from 29 league matches for a 9.59 average. Having narrowly lost out in the title chase, there was some consolation for the Pirates right at the end of the campaign when, having totalled 117 points, they lifted the Craven Shield, beating Peterborough (111) and Wolverhampton (96) in the three-legged final. For a second successive year, Poole could also boast having the World Champion in their ranks, as 'Ricko' followed in Mark Loram's tyre tracks and swept to victory in the Grand Prix series ahead of Jason Crump. Just for good measure, he repeated his success ahead of Crump in 2002, taking his tally to five titles and putting himself just one adrift of the legendary Ivan Mauger in terms of the most World Championships gained by one rider. Such was his dominance of the series that he virtually just had to turn up for the final round at the Telstra Stadium in Sydney, Australia on 26 October.

For the Pirates, Tony had a marvellous campaign, netting 11 maximums (10 full and 1 paid) on his way to 399 league points and a huge 10.99 average – the highest of his British career. In spite of his herculean efforts, Poole slipped back to fourth spot in the Elite League, but there was some silverware to celebrate at the death when, with 114 points, they retained the Craven Shield, defeating Ipswich (109) and Coventry (101) over three legs.

In 2003, the Pirates were rebuilt, with multi-Australian Champion Leigh Adams and Czech ace Lukas Dryml lending heat-leader support to Rickardsson in a particularly potent spearhead. With Gary Havelock moving on to Peterborough, the ultra-professional Swede was elected as the new club skipper and it really surprised nobody when Poole went on to win the Elite League and Knock-Out Cup. Making it a clean sweep, they scooped the British League Cup as well, although Tony didn't ride in that particular competition. His contribution to the league triumph was 263 points from 23 matches and a substantial 9.63 average. In the Grand Prix, he occupied third place in the final analysis, behind new Champion Nicki Pedersen and runner-up for a third year on the trot, Jason Crump. In terms of overall Grand Prix records, 'Ricko' is way out on his own, however, having won 12 of the 61 consecutive rounds he appeared in between 1995 and 2003.

Tony was still with the Pirates at the start of 2004, when he again showed tremendous form. There was, however, a shock in store for everyone at Poole when, in mid-April, he announced he was to quit the British scene to spend more time with his wife and family. The promoters made sure the Swedish great's farewell would be an occasion to remember while, with an eye on business, they also signed Australian ace Ryan Sullivan as his replacement. The date of 28 April marked the emotion-charged occasion of Rickardsson's final appearance in the Skull and Crossbones race-jacket and he bowed out with 10+2 points in a 49-42 victory. Co-promoter Matt Ford summed up the feelings of all the Wimborne Road regulars when he stated: 'Tony has been the man responsible for turning Poole into the speedway equivalent of Manchester United. We have been the team that everyone wants to beat.'

Tony departed to continue plying his trade in Swedish and Polish league racing, as well as the Grand Prix, and it is certainly not inconceivable that he could yet equal and ultimately beat Ivan Mauger's record of six World crowns. Many other successes have come his way in a glittering career, including a couple of victories in the Elite League Riders' Championship (1998 and 2002), while internationally he has helped Sweden to glory in the World Team Cup (1994 and 2000) and the World Pairs Final (1993).

Born: 23 July 1965, Swindon, Wiltshire

Competition	Matches	Points
League	189	1,272
Knock-Out Cup	24	159
Others	60	348
Three- and four-team tournaments	25	124
Pirates total	298	1,903

Alun John Rossiter, known throughout the speedway world as 'Rosco', has been associated with his hometown track, Swindon, throughout the majority of his life. Indeed, as a nipper he was first taken to a meeting at Blunsdon by his parents, and it is fair to say that right from day one he was fascinated by everything he saw. Although only knee-high to a grasshopper, Alun became mascot to the Wiltshire side at just four years of age and very soon was as popular with the supporters as the riders who wore the colours of the team. In his special position at Swindon, the young Rosco watched, listened and most importantly learned, and it must have come as no surprise whatsoever when he informed his parents that he wanted, one day, to become a speedway rider. The first step towards achieving this ambition saw him take up cycle speedway locally, with him described as a lad who was not particularly natural as a rider, but one who was very determined and prepared to work hard. This, of course, was something he always displayed in abundance when he finally made it as a speedway rider proper.

During the early 1980s, Swindon had a rich vein of junior talent, with a number of enthusiasts banding together to form a club which subsequently worked hard to raise funds so that this crop of youngsters could obtain as much racing experience as possible. Alun was one of the keenest in the group and through sheer determination he eventually came good, developing his own attacking style of racing. It was in 1982 that Exeter promoter Peter Oakes was short of a rider for a National League fixture at Crayford on 5 October and was persuaded to give Rosco a chance. The youngster grasped the opportunity to net 2+2 points, and just thirteen days later he rode in his first match for the senior Swindon side, ironically at Exeter, in the Martin Hewlett Benefit meeting, when he recorded a single point from his only start.

In 1983, besides appearing in the odd match for Swindon, Rossiter had a full and successful season with Exeter, helping them to lift the Knock-Out Cup. The following year saw him switch to Weymouth and he had a wonderful term, scoring 281 points for a huge National League average of 9.23. He also enjoyed plenty of additional opportunities when 'doubling-up' with Swindon, racing in 19 league matches and averaging exactly 4.00.

In 1985, Alun boldly asked to be considered for a full-time slot at his first love, Swindon, and his request was granted. Whilst it was tough, he never gave up trying and stuck to his task to average 4.13 from 20 league matches. Given his relative inexperience and considering it was his first full term in the top-flight, Rossiter was quite hard on himself and expressed disappointment at his end-of-term figure, thinking he ought to have done better.

In order to further his experience he spent 1986 on loan to Coventry and, riding under the promotion of the late Charles Ochiltree, this proved to be a very good move for him. Alun really got his head down, endeared himself to the hordes of Bees supporters and upped his average to precisely 5.00, remaining ever-present throughout the 20-match league programme for a second successive season.

He quickly returned to the fold at Swindon in 1987, when he produced several match-winning performances to post an average of 6.00, this amazingly being the third time in four seasons that he had posted an exact figure in the British League! His progress halted somewhat in 1988, for although he managed to net 196 points, his league average dropped a shade to 5.75.

It came as quite a surprise in 1989 when the Blunsdon faithful learned that he had been transferred to National League Poole. Rosco had actually first appeared in the Pirates colours as far back as 18 April 1984, when scoring 4+1 points in a League Cup match at home to Ipswich, but this was a new chapter in his career and he was to end up holding the Dorset club almost as close to his heart as Swindon. At Wimborne Road his special talents were immediately harnessed by the promoters for the good of the Pirates as they appointed him skipper. His ability to motivate team-mates, never minding if he himself was dropped from a race for the good of the side, created an excellent spirit within the pits. Poole had a wonderful season, culminating in them winning the Championship and only just missing out on the double when Berwick got the better of them in the Knock-Out Cup final. Of course, the Australian spearhead of Leigh Adams and Craig Boyce was pretty powerful in itself, but many a commentator made a point of stating just how big a part Alun's captaincy had played in the team's success. His on-track contribution was also noteworthy since he appeared in the full quota of 34 league matches, registering 291 points for an average of 8.08.

The next year went even better for the Dorset side as Rossiter steered his troops not only to back-to-back Championships, but also a final success over Middlesbrough in the Knock-Out Cup. The Swindonian enjoyed an even better campaign personally, scoring 324 points and raising his league average to 8.86.

Following an idea put forward to the BSPA by Poole promoter Mervyn Stewkesbury, the two leagues amalgamated in 1991, and the Pirates joined the new First Division. However, a series of knocks restricted Alun's appearances and affected his scoring, resulting in him being displaced by Peter Jeffery. He regained form and fitness with King's Lynn in 1992, but a change of circumstances at the Norfolk club saw him return to Poole in August, replacing the Sheffield-bound Tony Langdon.

The Pirates' promotion took over at relegated Swindon in 1993, and it was little surprise when the inspirational Rosco was installed as skipper of his hometown club. He began the campaign on fire, blasting to a 15-point maximum for the Robins in the season's opening challenge match versus Exeter at Blunsdon on 27 March. Despite not sustaining that kind of form, he still had a very good season, accumulating a total of 263 league points for an average of 7.44. Alun was then recalled to the 'Pirate Ship' for two years, during which time he filled the role of back-up boy to the heat-leaders and did his job exceptionally well.

In 1996, he initially had a spell with Peterborough, prior to rejoining Exeter in June, but his season ended abruptly on 2 September when a nasty crash at the County Ground left him with a fractured sternum and rib injuries. In 1997, Swindon boss Peter Toogood asked Alun to complete his side for the first season of Elite League racing. He duly rode his heart out, gleaning 111 points for an average of 4.49 before a knee injury effectively ended his season in August.

Continuing injury problems saw him complete just 2 league matches for the Robins in 1998, and there was more misfortune for the chirpy Rosco when his Testimonial meeting twice fell victim to rain. Keen to race again, he returned to the saddle with Oxford in 1999, before finally managing to stage his long-awaited Testimonial at Poole on 29 March 2000, when a host of leading stars turned out to pay tribute. He went on to represent both Wolverhampton and Poole that year, before

determined to do better in the second one. He was as good as his word too, and was riding well in the second heat, when Jernej Kolenko of King's Lynn lost control on the pits bend, sending Poole's Henrik Gustafsson crashing into Rosco. The Pirates guest rider piled into the safety fence and was a long time receiving medical attention. He slowly got to his feet and virtually staggered to the pits before climbing aboard his steed for the restart. Having made a good getaway, Alun, on borrowed machinery, was leading the re-run until the fourth bend when he pulled off the circuit and collapsed on the centre green. It was obvious he was very badly hurt, with a serious knee injury later diagnosed. That was the end of his season, and ultimately his career, with the knee remaining troublesome to this day. Just how he managed to get to his feet, return to the pits and even ride for a lap in the rerun was a complete mystery. As co-author Glynn Shailes put it on many occasions, 'he must have been on auto-pilot'.

Rosco wasn't lost to the sport though, as he became a regular visitor to Poole during 2003 and was also still very much part of the scene at Swindon, where he could be found working in the pits on race nights as mechanic to Olly Allen. At the beginning of November that year, Swindon promoter Peter Toogood concluded a deal that saw Terry Russell become club owner at Blunsdon, with the incoming boss immediately announcing that the Robins would compete in the Elite League in 2004. Come the end of the month, the Alun Rossiter story came full circle as he was installed as both promoter and team manager at Swindon. His amazing journey had seen him assume almost every possible role at the club, that of mascot, rider, captain, announcer, presenter, mechanic, training instructor, promoter and team manager, all before the age of forty!

again linking with Wolves in May 2001. A struggle for points ensued, but it was a different story when he answered an SOS call from Swindon in July, and he went on to attain a 7.24 average from 20 league matches. Despite not being retained, Alun was on hand to again help out the Robins in a couple of Premier Trophy matches at the start of 2002.

He later had a short spell with Trelawny, going down a storm with the Cornish fans, before accepting an offer to renew his acquaintance with Oxford. Disaster was to strike on 26 August though, when he accepted an offer to once more don a Pirates race-jacket in a double-header of league fare against King's Lynn at Wimborne Road. Following an off-colour performance in the first match he was

Born: 27 February 1958, Carshalton, Surrey

Competition	Matches	Points
League	292	2,844½
Knock-Out Cup	28	241
Others	78	732
Three- and four-team tournaments	45	332
Pirates total	**443**	**4,149½**

Early in 1979, Steven Schofield began his speedway career under the guidance of Gordon Kennett at an Eastbourne training school, prior to further honing his skills at Hackney. The following year, he continued on a sharp learning curve at Weymouth, although he was not without racing experience when he arrived at Radipole Lane, since he was already a grass-tracker of note. The date of his first meeting on the shale is recorded as 8 July 1980, when, as one of the reserves, he scored 2 points in the Seyco Soft Drinks Trophy at the Dorset venue. The diminutive rider was to have just a single outing in the Wildcats team that year, making what was his National League debut at Boston on 21 September, when he netted 2 points in a 44-34 defeat.

In 1981, Steve managed to force his way into the side on a regular basis and in a season of progress he netted 111 points from 27 league matches for an average of 5.42. Meanwhile, in his other chosen two-wheeled sport, he showed his mettle to win the 350cc British Grass-track Championship for what was a second successive year. It was in fact a title he would go on and retain every year up to and including 1986, making it seven straight victories in a row!

Schofield remained with Weymouth throughout the 1982 and 1983 seasons, raising his league average to 8.85 in the latter year. His sterling efforts also helped the Wildcats to reach the Knock-Out Cup final, although in a gripping encounter they went down by the narrowest of margins, losing 96-95 on aggregate to Exeter. Having assisted British League clubs on a number of occasions during the previous two seasons, Steve decided the time was right for a full-time move into top-flight rac-ing and he duly linked with Wolverhampton for the 1984 campaign. Unfortunately, he was involved in a nasty accident in a league match versus Poole at Monmore Green on 16 April, when he received broken ribs, a crushed vertebrae and lung injuries. That was to signal the end of his season but, bravely, he hauled himself back into the saddle to try again with the West Midlanders in 1985. Happily, he had an injury-free year and, racing against the sport's elite, he registered 79 league points for a satisfactory 5.37 average. Meanwhile in Dorset, his former bosses at Weymouth, Mervyn Stewkesbury and Pete Ansell, had moved their operation to Poole. In what was a marvellous year, the relocated Wildcats finished as runners-up to Ellesmere Port in the chase for the National League Championship. The ambitious promoters hoped to go one better in 1986 and a major move towards achieving their aim was tempting Schofield to come back under their wing.

From day one, the pint-sized racer showed just how pleased he was to be riding for Poole. His club debut occurred on 28 March and he

head position in the entire National League figures. Individually, he produced an outstanding performance in the prestigious Blue Riband on 9 August, tallying 14 points to take the title from Mildenhall's Mel Taylor.

A surprise was in store for the fans down Dorset way in 1989, as the Pirates' management sought to build a balanced side within the rules. They just couldn't fit Steve into any of their favoured combinations, with the result that he went on loan to Hackney. There was no let-up in his scoring though, as he comfortably held on to his number one position in the league, courtesy of a huge 10.60 average. He made a couple of favourable sorties back to Wimborne Road during the year as well, firstly winning the Echo Pairs Classic with Hackney team-mate Andy Galvin on 18 July and then successfully defending the Blue Riband ahead of Poole's Alastair Stevens on 1 August.

Still with the Kestrels in 1990, Schofield attained a 10.44 average and there was glory along the way when he partnered Andy Galvin to victory in the National League Pairs Championship at Glasgow on 17 June. Steve was subsequently recalled by the Pirates upon their elevation to the new First Division in 1991, having twice won the league (1989 and 1990) and also gained a Knock-Out Cup triumph (1990) in his absence. Anyway, his ability shone through amidst the higher echelons and he could be well satisfied with a 7.93 average, having garnered 222 points from the 24-match league programme.

Schofield's consistent points-gathering became a normal feature of Poole meetings throughout the early part of the decade, and in 1994 he played a key role as the Pirates raced away to win the Division One title by 15 clear points from Eastbourne. His contribution was 330 points and an 8.04 league average, as he ably backed up the heat-leader trio of Jason Crump (9.35), Craig Boyce (9.14) and Lars Gunnestad (8.83). The Dorseteers collected further silverware in the Four-Team Championship at Peterborough on 7 August, when a total of 28 points gave them victory over Cradley Heath (20), Eastbourne (15) and Coventry (9), with Steve's tally being half-a-dozen points on the day. His great loyalty to

marked the occasion by plundering a faultless 12-point full-house, as his new side defeated Exeter 48-30 in an Easter Trophy fixture. It's quite appropriate to say Steve was a revelation over the course of the season, since he compiled a total of 439 points from a full quota of 38 league matches for a mighty 10.45 average. Despite this and the top-end support of Kevin Smith (9.36) and Martin Yeates (8.80), the Wildcats again had to settle for second place in the final table, 6 points adrift of Eastbourne.

In 1987, the side reverted back to their traditional Pirates nickname, but they didn't enjoy such a good term on track and dropped back to eighth spot in the league. The wee man from Surrey had another excellent year, however, and in posting a 9.62 average, he remained the club's kingpin.

Remarkably, for the third time in four seasons, Poole were to finish as league runners-up in 1988, with the title going to a powerful Hackney outfit. 'Scoie' was not only the team's top man once more, but in recording 357½ points and an average of 10.37 he occupied the

Poole, and indeed the Stewkesbury/Ansell promotional duo, was rewarded in 1995 when a large crowd attended a worthy Testimonial at Wimborne Road on 30 July. The meeting saw the Grass-track Elite defeat the Speedway Supremes 51-33, with a host of stars on show to honour the deserved beneficiary. The season had heralded a new 21-team Premier League and although the Pirates slipped to twelfth place, Scoie put together a tremendous term to yield 302 league points and an 8.30 average.

One further season of Premier League activity followed in 1996, and Steve was still identified in a Skull and Crossbones racejacket for the inaugural year of the Elite League in 1997. This was a tough sphere of racing and while his scoring was understandably reduced it came as a blow when his bosses made the difficult decision to replace him in August. Regrettably, that brought the curtain down on a wonderful career in the blue and white colours, which had seen him accrue a grand total of 4,149½ points in all competitions for the Pirates – a record that is only bettered by Craig Boyce.

Oxford joined the Elite League in 1998 under the new promotional team of Steve and Vanessa Purchase, with Terry Russell also on board to assist in their initial year in the hot-seat. With the help of the BSPA a competitive side was assembled and one of their signings was the experienced Schofield, who duly took the role of skipper. Few realised then, but it was to be his final year of speedway and he went out with a useful league average of 5.54.

During his shale days, he was capped by England and also made representative appearances for the National League. He was a multi-finalist in the World Long-track Championship, and on the grass he was British 500cc Champion in 1988. Unable to find a speedway berth in 1999, Steve took a day job and raced on the grass at weekends. It was in one such meeting – the Bonfire Burn-up at Collier Street, Yalding, near Tonbridge on 7 November – that his time in the saddle ended in the most unfortunate fashion. He had qualified for the final, but just after the eight-strong field had left the gate he was involved in a terrible pile-up, which left him unconscious with both legs broken and also pelvic injuries. It took Scoie the best part of four years to overcome the effects of the accident, but during the preparation of this book came the good news that he has finally been cleared medically to begin working again.

Born: 20 March 1946, Tonbridge, Kent

Competition	Matches	Points
League	186	2,001
Knock-Out Cup	15	171
Others	64	585
Three- and four-team tournaments	13	120
Pirates total	**278**	**2,877**

Malcolm Simmons began his career in speedway at a Rye House training school in 1963, and following some second-half rides at New Cross he linked with Provincial League Hackney Wick to net a tally of 79 league points. However, in 1964, with the Provincial League running outside the jurisdiction of the Speedway Control Board, both Malcolm and his Hawks team-mate Norman Hunter switched their allegiance to West Ham, a club that had reopened having last run in 1955. The Tonbridge boy scored just 13 points at National League level for the Hammers that year, but had impressed sufficiently to be retained in 1965, when the British League was formed. He did well too, and certainly played a part in the success of West Ham, who pipped fellow Londoners Wimbledon to the inaugural Championship. Indeed, the young Simmons remained ever-present over the 34-match league programme and accumulated 174 points for an impressive 6.16 average. Aside from that, he helped the Hammers to complete a glorious double, as they cruised to an aggregate 114-78 victory over Exeter in the Knock-Out Cup final. Remaining with West Ham in both 1966 and 1967, he posted league averages of 6.10 and 7.01 respectively, before a change of scenery saw him join King's Lynn.

For the next seven seasons (1968-1974), Malcolm and Terry Betts were neck-and-neck when it came to heading the Stars averages, with Simmons' best year occurring in 1973, when he recorded 399 points for a huge 10.39

league average. All told, he represented the Norfolk team in league activity on 223 occasions, scoring 2,112½ points along the way, and was sorely missed by their supporters when go-ahead Poole promoter Charles Knott made a successful bid that brought him to the South Coast in 1975.

The incoming man arrived at Wimborne Road as a genuine number one rider and over a six-year period he was to provide the club with sterling service. Malcolm's first season as a Pirate was nothing short of phenomenal as, in 31 league matches, he plundered 16 maximums (15 full and 1 paid) on his way to 344 points and an average of 10.39. Poole didn't enjoy the happiest of times on the domestic front, finishing fifteenth out of eighteen teams, but at least in Simmons they had a speedster who kept the fans' interest alive with his incredible performances. The prestigious individual meeting at Poole since 1970 had been the Blue Riband, and on 13 August, the leading Pirate produced a top drawer showing to take the coveted trophy ahead of Exeter's Scott Autrey.

'Super Simmo', as he had been dubbed by the good folk of Poole, supplied much more of the same in 1976, riding in 34 league matches to score 399 points and average 10.30. There were also another 11 maximums (8 full and 3 paid), and for a second successive year he was victorious in the Blue Riband, held on 8 September. Given the sheer level of his consistency, it is fair to say he WAS Poole Speedway and his popularity within the town had reached that of a superstar, with car stickers bearing his name to be found on every street.

Malcolm maintained his immaculate form for the Pirates in 1977, when a total of 299 points and 10 maximums (9 full and 1 paid) yielded a league average of 10.22. Meanwhile, for a third year on the trot, he took the opposition to the cleaners, scoring 14 points to win the Blue Riband ahead of Dave Jessup on 7 September. If anything, Simmons went even better in 1978, when he registered 358 points and 11 maximums (10 full and 1 paid) from 32 league matches for a mighty 10.78 average. Remarkably, on 9 August, he posted victory in the Blue Riband for a fourth straight season, defeating Ole Olsen in a title run-off after both had totalled 14 points.

In 1979, the legendary Knott family sold the Poole licence to Reg and Joan Fearman, and by comparison with the high standards Malcolm had set in the past, his statistical record for this year revealed quite a drop in fortunes. With 273 league points and an average of 8.93, he only just held onto his position as the club's number one, finishing marginally ahead of new young American Ron Preston (8.71). Having said that, it was still a good return from Simmo, and one that many other riders would have been delighted with.

Still with Poole in 1980, Malcolm became unsettled at one point and asked for a transfer, but later withdrew the request despite being replaced as club captain by Neil Middleditch. Things came to a head on 1 October, however, when Poole hosted the Sheba World Travel Best Pairs, and in the final heat he ran a third behind John Davis and Malcolm Holloway. The result put Davis and Holloway level on 18 points with the pairing of Ron Preston and Shawn Moran, although it was Preston who remained cool to defeat Davis in a subsequent title run-off. Simmons was later quoted as saying, 'A small section of the crowd, along with the management, accused me of not trying. That has never been my style, and hopefully it never will be.' The Poole linchpin then received a telegram informing him his services were no longer required by the club, with team manager Terry Chandler commenting, 'Simmons is finished with Poole, and this time there will be no going back.' It was a great pity considering all Malcolm had done for the club, and the value of his efforts was demonstrated by the fact that he still ended-up topping the Pirates end-of-term figures, with 274 points giving an increased league average of 9.40.

He subsequently went to Wimbledon, where he was to spend four seasons (1981-1984).

Simmo continued his career with Swindon in 1985, prior to a drop into the National League with former club Hackney in 1986. He was back at his brilliant best with the then-nicknamed Kestrels too, scoring 372 points for a league average of 9.71, with the year also seeing him make 4 league appearances for King's Lynn in the top-flight.

Hackney rejoined the British League in 1987, and Malcolm was happy to stay on board, but it was to turn into a year to forget. He missed just one of Hackney's 22 League Cup fixtures, averaging 5.46, but following the club's very first league match of the season, versus Swindon at Waterden Road on 31 July, he unluckily suffered a dislocated shoulder in a second-half accident. On 30 September, he took a couple of point-less and painful rides as he attempted a comeback at King's Lynn, and that appeared to be the end of his glittering career. However, he made a resumption with National League Arena-Essex in 1989, and in spite of a terrifying crash at Middlesbrough on 25 May, he did well to record a 7.45 league average from 14 matches.

Out of the blue, after seemingly being lost to the sport, Simmons surprisingly rode in a couple of Division One matches for King's Lynn in 1993, but since then, despite continuing to ride on grass, he has resisted all subsequent temptations of returning to the shale. With numerous England caps to his name, the highlights of an exceedingly long career were 3 World Final appearances (1975, 1976 and 1978), the best of which occurred at Katowice, Poland on 5 September 1976, when he totalled 13 points to finish as runner-up to fellow countryman Peter Collins. In the World Team Cup, he was a winner on four occasions, once with Great Britain (1973), and three times with England (1974, 1975 and 1977), while in the World Pairs Championship, he secured a hat-trick of victories, each time accompanied by different partners, namely John Louis (1976), Peter Collins (1977) and Gordon Kennett (1978). He also made 10 British Final appearances, once being crowned Champion when a 15-point maximum took him to victory at Coventry on 2 June 1976.

Born: 2 September 1948, Avesta, Sweden

Competition	Matches	Points
League	129	795
National Trophy	12	72
Others	47	245
Three- and four-team tournaments	7	21
Pirates total	**195**	**1,133**

Christer Sjosten was the younger brother of Soren, who graced the British racing scene between 1962 and 1978 and enjoyed many terrific seasons, particularly in his time with Belle Vue. After taking up the sport at his local track in 1969, Christer first came to ride here in the UK in 1971, when he joined British League Division One side Wembley. Having been in the speedway wilderness since the end of the 1956 campaign, the famous Lions had reopened the previous year under the promotion of Trevor Redmond and Bernard Cottrell. Despite only appearing in 6 league matches for the Middlesex club, the Swede revealed plenty of promise to score 16 points for a 4.21 average.

Wembley Stadium again closed its doors to speedway at the end of the season as the authorities were unable to guarantee regular use to the sport because of its many other commitments. Christer then had an even shorter stint with Exeter in 1972, when he

rode in just 3 league fixtures for 9 points and an average of 5.33. He clearly had talent but needed a full-time berth and this is exactly what happened the following term when he ventured to Scotland and linked with Coatbridge. A memorable day occurred on 27 April when he secured his first league maximum (12 points) in a home match versus Cradley United and he was to enjoy a successful season with the Tigers, totalling 185 points to yield a 6.44 average.

Unfortunately for Sjosten, the BSPA banned commuting Swedish riders in 1974, but the ruling was to only last for that one year before he, along with his compatriots, made a return. He then accepted a contract with Poole and duly made his club debut in a Champagne Stakes match against visiting Swindon on 19 March 1975, scoring 2+1 points. Christer got plenty of encouragement from the Wimborne Road faithful as the season wore on, and when all the dust had settled a tally of 155 points gave him a league average of 6.19 and third spot in the club's statistical run-down behind Malcolm Simmons (10.39) and Eric Broadbelt (7.50).

Welcomed back by the Pirates in 1976, he was an efficient performer, netting useful points in every match he rode. There were a couple of high spots along the way, the first of which came on 18 August in a British League match at home to Leicester. The Poole boys went on the rampage to slaughter their opponents 59-19, with the spectacular Sjosten helping himself to a 12-point full-house. Then, a week later, King's Lynn were the visitors to Dorset and he sped to another 4-ride maximum as the Pirates dismissed their visitors by a 55-23 scoreline. Come the season's end, he had totted up 208 points for a slightly increased league figure of 6.77, as he once more lent support to the top two of 'Simmo' (10.30) and Eric Broadbelt (7.14).

Christer was again included in the Poole septet in 1977, but his year was to be marred by a couple of nasty knocks which kept him on the sidelines for lengthy spells. The first happened in a British League match at Ipswich on 22 June, when he suffered broken bones in a foot and was out of action for the best part of six weeks. After returning to the saddle it was not long before he fractured an arm in a qualifying round for the Volkswagen/*Daily Mirror* Grand Prix at Hackney on 16 September. That brought his season to a premature end and although the Swede posted an average of exactly 8.00, the injuries had curtailed him to just 15 appearances in the 36-match league programme. Aside from registering a paid maximum (14+1) versus Exeter in a league match at Wimborne Road on 15 June, perhaps the most rewarding performance of a frustrating year occurred in his homeland when he partnered brother Soren to victory in the Swedish Pairs Championship.

Still with the Pirates in 1978, Christer put the disappointments of the previous season behind him as 193 points yielded a 7.18 average from 29 league matches. There was a consistent level of scoring about his game, littered with the odd exceptional showing and this form was recognised internationally when Sweden selected him for the Intercontinental Final of the World Team Cup, staged at Belle Vue on 18 June. The meeting saw England accumulate 33 points to take victory from Denmark (25), Sweden (23) and Australia (14), with Sjosten contributing 2 points while fellow Poole rider Malcolm Simmons recorded a tally of 11 for a triumphant home nation.

Christer made it five successive years with the Dorset side in 1979 and the club's enthusiastic supporters were happy to see him sporting the blue and white colours once more. His thrilling style not only made him popular but also courted injury and, not for the first time, he was out of action for a spell after crashing in a home British League match against Swindon on 25 July. Nevertheless, when he was fit and on song he was undoubtedly an asset to Poole. This was evident in an earlier match at Leicester on 26 June, when he accrued 11+2 points, although his efforts could not prevent a 40-38 defeat. When the figures were added up at the end of the season, the Swede had 144 league points and a 6.50 league average to his name, with the fans looking forward to more of the same full-throttle action in 1980.

Tragically, it wasn't to be. Sjosten decided to race in Australia during the winter season, but in a meeting at Brisbane Exhibition Speedway on 1 December, he unfortunately collided with a timber post and never regained consciousness, passing away in hospital five days later. His loss was a terrible blow and hit all at Poole Speedway hard. As a tribute and mark of respect, the Christer Sjosten Memorial meeting was held at Wimborne Road on 23 April 1980, when Swindon's Bob Kilby took victory with 14 points. Capped by Sweden on several occasions, Christer was a rider who, long before his fatal accident, had earned the respect of the Poole supporters and management for his wholehearted efforts on behalf of the team.

Born: 6 January 1927, Southampton, Hampshire

Competition	Matches	Points
League	250	1,541
National Trophy	46	360
Others	92	676
Three-team tournaments	1	6
Pirates total	**389**	**2,583**

Terence Frank Small joined Poole in 1949 as a young and highly promising rider, and went on to do great things as a Pirate. Prior to that, he had first taken an interest in motorcycles at the age of just ten years and later began racing on the local grass-tracks. During the latter part of the Second World War, Terry, who had served as a dispatch-rider, also enjoyed some racing on the sand-tracks of Egypt, once even finishing as runner-up in the All-Egypt Sand Racing Championship.

Linking with the 'Pirate Ship', he took his bow in the second half of a National Trophy tie versus Great Yarmouth at Wimborne Road on 23 May, when he ran a second to Frank Wheeler in the Stadium Scurry. After several weeks of second-half rides, and an appearance as reserve in the Lucky Stars Trophy, he made his debut in the Poole team on 11 July, when he netted 3+2 points from 2 starts in a home league match against Plymouth. In his second outing (heat 12), he finished as runner-up to team-mate Fred Pawson, and the strange circumstances surrounding this race are worth recalling. Plymouth rider Ivan Kessell was forced to pull out through engine failure, while his colleague Peter Robinson was excluded for boring. The flag marshal waved the black flag to indicate his exclusion, but all three remain-

ing riders mistakenly took this to mean the race had been stopped. However, having heard the shouts of encouragement from the terraces, the home duo continued on to collect a 5-0 advantage, with Pawson taking victory in a time of 103.2 seconds – nearly 27 seconds outside Billy Bales' then track record of 76.4! Small went on to hold his place in the side, finishing the season with a tally of 59 points from 27 league matches and his whole-hearted efforts were duly recognised when he was presented with the Freshman's Tankard.

In 1950, after a poor start to the season, the Pirates suddenly found their feet to eventually end the campaign in second place, 5 points behind Champions Oxford. Terry's development was steady throughout the year and he held his place in the side on merit, notching 127 league points from 27 meetings. During the winter months, things looked rather bleak for Poole Speedway until Len Matchan and Geoffrey Bravery took over the promotional reins, and thus began a period of track success, not only for the club but also for Terry Small as an individual. The Pirates swung into action with a challenge match against a visiting Norwich side on 26 March 1951, and in a 44-40 victory, he recorded a couple of storming wins on his way to 9 points. This marked the beginning of a truly fantastic season for the Southampton-born racer as he went on to become the club's second heat-leader behind Ken Middleditch, accumulating 307 points from 35 Division Three matches for a super 9.60 average. Along the way, on 14 May, he thundered around the Poole circuit in a league encounter with St Austell, clocking 73.6 seconds to equal Ken Middleditch's track record.

His excellent form saw that he was capped at England 'C' level in all 5 Test matches against New Zealand, as well as in all 3 such meetings versus Sweden. He was also nominated to challenge Aldershot's Trevor Redmond for the Division Three Match Race Championship, and he took the speedy Kiwi to three legs before finally admitting defeat. With the form of Middleditch and Small, not to mention that of Tony Lewis, Brian Crutcher, Bill Holden *et al*, Poole swept to the league title and were rewarded with promotion to the Second Division. Moving up had no effect on the Pirates, and the bandwagon just rolled on, with the men in blue and white romping to the 1952 Championship courtesy of an 8-point margin from nearest challengers, Coventry. Terry's contribution to the success was a haul of 333 points from a full quota of 44 league matches and a healthy 8.75 average. He subsequently wintered in New Zealand to further his experience and represented England in a Test match at Auckland, scoring 6 points in a 47-24 defeat.

It was to be another excellent term for Poole in 1953, although in the end they surrendered the Championship by a single point to Coventry. It is well documented that Brian Crutcher left for Wembley after 10 league matches, but it is inconceivable to imagine that they wouldn't have retained the title had the 'Nipper' stayed on board. Still, Small enjoyed another good year in the famous Skull and Crossbones race-jacket, registering 260 points from 31 matches to finish as runner-up to Ken Middleditch (292) in the Pirates list of league scorers. Happily, he had been mainly accident-free during his career up to that point, but that changed in 1954 when he suffered a series of injuries. While the ideal situation would have been to rest and recover fully, Terry just kept on riding in order to do his bit for Poole. As a result, he lost form and only rarely did supporters catch a glimpse of him at his best. Despite the fact he was only able to clock up 73 points from 13 matches in a reduced league programme, the Pirates again managed to finish as runners-up, with 'demoted' Bristol claiming the Championship, having retained all their old First Division team members.

Thankfully, Small recovered full fitness for 1955 and showed much of his old sparkle to record 236 league points from 31 matches. Poole simply dominated the Second Division and raced to the title ahead of Coventry for what was their third Championship success in five glorious seasons. There was only one place the Pirates could go in 1956, and that was to Division One. Naturally, some riders with top-flight experience were signed to boost the side's chances at the higher level and at one stage, albeit only for a week or so, they actually topped the table. Terry found the pace a tad too hot, this being borne out by end-of-term figures of 70 points from 20 matches, which yielded a league average of 5.40. However, it's fair to say that, Ken Middleditch apart, most of the boys who had ridden so well in the Second Division were in the same boat and found the points hard to come by.

Regrettably, in 1957, Poole actually closed and their riders were re-allocated elsewhere, yet surprisingly no team seemed to want Terry Small. Eventually, Jack Crutcher received permission to run a series of open-licence meetings at Wimborne Road, while Vic Gooden also ran a couple of his Rayleigh side's league matches at the Dorset venue. Small was on hand to ride for the aptly named Rayleigh Pirates and he also appeared in 2 challenge matches for Poole. A further England cap also came his way, when he represented his country in Holland, scoring 9 points in a 46-36 victory in the first Test match at Hengelo.

In 1958, Vic Gooden promoted the fortunes of Poole, as they resumed in a ten-team National League, with Small back on board. Unfortunately, he wasn't the rider of old and could only attain 36 points from 10 league matches. Things were much the same in 1959, when he scored 40 league points from a dozen meetings and also represented Poole in the National Reserve League. At the end of the campaign, he called it a day and one report in the speedway press suggested that a painful lump, apparently containing a link of bike chain, on one of his legs had taken its toll. Nevertheless, in an eleven-year span, Terry had been a Poole man through and through, and during that time his film star looks had made him especially popular with the many female fans of the Pirates.

Born: 29 July 1961, Canterbury, Kent

Competition	Matches	Points
League	189	1,278
Knock-Out Cup	12	72
Others	102	767½
Four-team tournaments	14	110
Pirates total	**317**	**2,227½**

Kevin James Smith always looked destined for a career in speedway, since he was the mascot at Canterbury throughout their opening season of Second Division racing in 1968. Aged just seven, he also took up junior grass-track racing that same year, becoming a member of the Kent Youth Grass-track Riders' Association. He took to the sport like a duck to water, going on to complete a hat-trick of victories at schoolboy level in the British Grass-track Championship (1971, 1972 and 1973). His skill on the grass was further emphasised when he was later crowned Club Champion of the Kent Youth MCC on three occasions (1974, 1976 and 1977).

It was only natural that Kevin would move on to speedway and he took his first such rides at Hackney in 1977, prior to linking with the junior Rye House side in 1978. Having shown terrific form for the Hoddesdon-based outfit, he was loaned out to Weymouth and made his National League debut at Crayford on 20 May, when he scored a single point in a 49-28 defeat. He was to make just one further league appearance for the Wildcats before he was recalled to ride for the senior Rye House team, as and when required. By the end of the term, Smith had ridden in 18 league matches for the Rockets, with a total of 63 points giving him an impressive 4.97 average.

In 1979, as a regular in the Hertfordshire side, his outstanding progress was much commented on in speedway circles. Indeed, in what was only his first full season in the sport, Kevin accumulated 263 points from 34 league matches to yield an average of 8.54. A highlight was a first full maximum (15 points) in a home match against Nottingham on 8 July, and he was to notch 4 more full-houses (3 full and 1 paid) before the close of the campaign. The year also saw him gain British League experience with Hackney, for whom he achieved a 4.80 average from 5 matches.

Smith produced many more excellent performances in 1980, remaining ever-present over Rye House's 38-match National League programme to net 283 points and an 8.61 average. A further 4 outings were made for Hackney in the higher sphere of domestic racing and at the end of the season he unsurprisingly decided his future lay in the British League. Eventually, Poole were to secure the signature of the highly-rated youngster and a substantial transfer fee (reported to be £10,000) changed hands.

His Pirates debut subsequently occurred in a League Cup encounter versus King's Lynn at Wimborne Road on 1 April 1981, and in a fabulous start he recorded 11 points from 5 rides in a hard-fought 48½-47½ victory. The points were to flow freely as the League Cup competition progressed and it wasn't long before the management and supporters realised that the money shelled out had been very well spent. Early prominent performances included a paid maximum (11+1) in only his second home match against Hackney on 8 April, and the very next night he produced a wonder-show at Wimbledon, plundering 17 points from 7 rides.

This high scoring was recognised internationally when he was selected to ride at reserve for England in the second Test match versus America at Poole on 29 April. He failed to open his account from the single ride he took, but nonetheless it was an honour to have been capped by his country. He was later picked as reserve for England in the first Test against Denmark at Hackney on 12 June, but on that occasion he wasn't called upon to ride. Prior to that he had raced in the British Final at Coventry on 3 June, but he enjoyed little luck on the night and finished up with just a couple of points. Getting back to Kevin's first year with Poole, his scoring wasn't quite so high during the league campaign, although it should be remembered he was riding on many of the away circuits for the first time. Even so, he still racked up 164 points for a solid 6.89 average from 27 such matches. Adding to his experience, during the 1981/82 winter, he toured Australia with Young England, appearing in all 5 Test matches, his best tally being 3 points in a 54-54 draw at Mildura on 13 December.

Much was expected from the Canterbury boy in 1982 and initially it looked as though he was making headway, but then, like many riders before, he seemed to 'stand still'. The fact that Poole floundered at the wrong end of the league table didn't help, and to cap it all he was to end the season nursing a broken arm. The final statistics saw the Pirates propping up the league, with Smith contributing 135 points from 27 meetings. Nobody doubted he had the talent to reach the top, although it was a case of 'as you were' in 1983, when he registered 156 points from 26 matches, as Poole again struggled and finally finished thirteenth out of the fifteen British League teams.

The tough times continued for the Dorset side in 1984, culminating in the promoting company, Poole Stadium Ltd, going into liquidation in January 1985. Kevin lost form completely and actually quit for a short spell. By the end of the season, he was out on loan to Swindon, for whom he rode in just 3 league matches. For Poole, he had recorded 78 points from 23 British League meetings – figures which emphasised the slump in his scoring.

There were times during the winter when the Pirates supporters wondered whether it was the end of their beloved club. However, the Weymouth management, Mervyn Stewkesbury and Pete Ansell, saved the day when they moved their operation into Wimborne Road. They introduced National League racing to the Poole faithful, with the side adopting the old Weymouth moniker of 'Wildcats'. The incoming bosses wanted Smith and reputedly paid a fee of £6,250 to the BSPA for his services. With his appetite rekindled, Kevin began the campaign in superb fashion, romping to a 12-point maximum in the opening meeting, a challenge match versus visiting Milton Keynes on 5 April. He followed that up with a 5-ride full-house in the Easter Trophy at Exeter three days later and the tone was set for the year. Poole came within a whisker of winning the league title, missing out by a single point to Ellesmere Port. Smith played a full part in the chase for the Championship, appearing in all 36 matches to post a 9.38 average, having accrued 350 points and 9 maximums (5 full and 4 paid). During the year, he shaved half-a-second off the track record at Wimborne Road, firstly clocking 63.4 seconds on 25 June to beat Gordon Kennett's previous best of 63.5. Then, on 30 July, he lowered his own record to 63.1 seconds, before being timed at 63.0 dead in a league match against Wimbledon on 24 September.

The Wildcats continued in the same vein in 1986, when they were always up with the league leaders. They eventually ended up in the runner-up spot again, 6 points adrift of Eastbourne, but it could rightly be said that an injury sustained by Kevin effectively put paid to their chances. This happened in a Knock-Out Cup tie at home to Arena-Essex on 29 April, when he sustained a complex fracture of the fibula and was out of action until 8 July. When fit, it was another excellent year for the speedy racer, with 200 points equating to a league average of 9.36.

The 1987 season was to be his last in the saddle, and despite producing worthwhile league figures of 195 points and a 7.33 average for the traditionally retitled Pirates, he gave up the sport and retired. With a club total of 2,227½ points, Kevin holds eleventh position in the list of all-time top scorers for the Skull and Crossbones.

Born: 11 July 1942, Hanworth, Feltham, Middlesex

Competition	Matches	Points
League	465	2,760
National Trophy & Knock-Out Cup	34	214
Others	116	614
Four-team tournaments	5	23
Pirates total	**620**	**3,611**

Peter Smith was to become one of a very small band of riders who spent their entire racing career with Poole Pirates. When he was just nine years of age, he got his first taste of live action at Wembley, and having become a staunch supporter of the famous Lions, he subsequently became a cycle speedway competitor. Following the closure of Wembley after the 1956 season, he went on to be a regular on the terraces at Wimbledon, where he became friends with young novice Roy Trigg, and after purchasing a speedway bike and leathers for the princely sum of £25, he began practising in a local sandpit. This wasn't a great success, although it was memorable inasmuch as he often crashed into bushes and all but climbed a tree on one occasion!

He wasn't put off, however, and made up his mind to get further training at Rye House, where he was helped by Mike Broadbanks. When they were short of riders for a Best Pairs meeting at the Hoddesdon raceway on 23 April 1961, Pete was called upon to part-

ner Geoff Mudge. While the Australian went about the business of compiling a 4-ride maximum, Smith notched a couple of third-place points and their combined efforts were sufficient to win the meeting, giving the rookie an initial speedway success. Later, at Easter time in 1962, he journeyed with Roy Trigg to Poole, not knowing that his good mate had arranged for him to have a second-half outing. Following that, he continued to learn his trade with after-the-meeting rides at Wimborne Road throughout the year and was to actually make his first appearance for the Pirates in what was billed as a 'Four-a-Side Challenge Match' at Rye House on 12 August. With a total of 41 points, Stoke won the meeting ahead of Poole (38), Rye House (24) and Wolverhampton (15), and although Pete's contribution might have been but a single point, it was the first of many he would register for the Skull and Crossbones.

He had clearly shown enough promise to stake a claim for a regular team berth, and although he missed the first 2 Southern League matches at home and away against Exeter in 1963, he was included in the side for a similar meeting at Hackney on 24 April. The Pirates went on to register a 45-33 victory in the match, with the new boy notching 1 point from 2 starts. He was to go on and appear in 23 league matches over the course of the season and a tally of 84 points represented a sound beginning. Highlights occurred in home matches against Sheffield (7+2), Hackney (7+3), Rayleigh (7+2) and Stoke (7+1), and although it was harder going on the road, he did attain a 6+1 return at Rayleigh on 7 September.

Having so much enjoyed the countryside of Dorset and the friendliness of the people too, Smith made an important decision at the end of the campaign, moving from his London base to Poole. The sport was shrouded in politics in 1964 and it was that often-difficult second full year for the youngster, who accumulated 69 points from 21 Provincial League matches. He still came up with some handy scores, like 7+2 points at Glasgow on 29 May, but didn't make the hoped-for leap forward. All that changed in 1965, however, with the birth of the British League. He was consistency personified and ended the season in sparkling form, hitting scores of 7+2, 7+3 and 7+4 in home matches against Swindon, Sheffield and Coventry respectively. Those performances took him to a season's total of 127 points from 32 league matches for an extremely healthy 5.54 average.

There was much more of the same in 1966, when his away form generally improved too. He recorded a first full maximum (15 points) against Exeter in the opening meeting of the year, an Easter Trophy fixture at Wimborne Road on 8 April, and went on to yield a league average of 5.70, having recorded 125 points from 30 matches. Although it was another steady year for Pete, local pressman Colin Smith of the *Evening Echo* described him thus: 'Brilliant at times, disappointing at others and never quite reaching the heights that seemed within his grasp.' The journalist did, however, compliment his namesake by reporting: 'Smith's spirit never suffered and Pete's most vital contributions often came when they were most needed by the team.'

In 1967, his performances went up a gear and he was to become perhaps the best 'back-up' man in the business, as he lent solid support to the heat-leader trio of Gote Nordin, Geoff Mudge and Ronnie Genz. This is borne out by the statistics, which show him as an ever-present throughout Poole's 36 league matches and with a total of 171 points, his average improved to a 6.33 figure. The development continued in 1968, when his 'easy on the eye' style saw him become Poole's third heat-leader behind Bill Andrew and Geoff Mudge. The Dorseteers slumped to seventeenth place in the league table, but that didn't stop Smith

from totting up 266 points, as he again appeared in every one of the 36 league matches for an average of 7.51.

So to 1969 and the year when it all came right for the Poole Pirates. The boys in blue and white stormed to the British League Division One Championship by a 6-point margin from Belle Vue, and they owed much to Pete Smith, who brilliantly rose all the way to the number one position in the club averages with a huge 9.52 figure. This was achieved with 282½ points from 32 league meetings, including no fewer than 8 maximums (4 full and 4 paid). *Evening Echo* correspondent Colin Smith commented that having responded to the excellent leadership of skipper Geoff Mudge, Pete was 'at last blossoming into the top-class rider that he always promised to become'. International caps also came his way during the year, against Australia, New Zealand and Scotland, and despite only scoring 2 points on the big night, he represented the Pirates in the British League Riders' Championship, staged at Belle Vue on 18 October.

Along came the 1970s, with the man from Middlesex still an essential part of the Poole set-up. In the cut and thrust of top-flight British League racing, high scores were commonplace for Pete as the years passed by, with seasonal points totals of 255 (1970), 261 (1971), 255 (1972) and 246 (1973). In terms of averages he never quite scaled the heights of 1969, but nevertheless his levels of consistency were truly amazing. During that period, as might have been expected, there were many other achievements of note. For instance, in 1971, he took over as Poole captain following the departure of Geoff Mudge, and gained more England caps versus the Soviet Union. In 1972 he raced for England against Norway/Denmark, and in 1973 he appeared for Great Britain versus Poland, and also reached the British Final, scoring 5 points in the prestigious event at Sheffield on 21 June. The year also saw him make a second appearance in the BLRC at Belle Vue, but he unfortunately ended the meeting with a 'duck'.

In 1974, he knocked-up another 214 league points in the cause of Poole, while also making a further appearance for England against

and fittingly it was Pete and team-mate Colin Gooddy who came out on top with a combined tally of 27 points. Clearly inspired by the events of the year, he enjoyed a better campaign domestically to net an increased total of 185 points for a 6.16 league average.

Poole were unfairly described by the media as an 'ageing' side in 1977, when the long-serving Smith embarked on his fifteenth full season as a Pirate. He was used mainly at reserve and it often proved a godsend to have a reliable man occupying such a position in the line-up. His figures for the term were 117 points from 34 league matches and, although he was still capable of doing a job, he called it a day for keeps.

His career with Poole was legendary, having risen from a raw novice to pile up many, many points over a long period of time, while also establishing a club record of 620 appearances in all competitions. He was subsequently coaxed back on to a bike for one of Barry Briggs' Golden Greats meetings on 13 September 2000, when the Wimborne Road faithful enjoyed a fabulous evening of nostalgia. To this day, Pete can often be spotted enjoying the racing from Poole's wonderful glass-fronted grandstand; understandably, he just can't keep away from the place that holds such marvellous memories!

Sweden. A tough start to 1975 saw Smith retire in May, but he resumed racing in mid-term and still managed to net a total of 103 points from 25 league matches. He was into his thirties by this time of course, yet was still a more-than-useful team man and his efforts were rewarded with a deserved Testimonial in 1976. The crowds duly turned out in force for his special meeting, a Best Pairs tournament, on 8 August,

Born: 21 November 1921, Poole, Dorset

Competition	Matches	Points
League	157	921½
National Trophy	38	268
Others	49	297
Three- and four-team tournaments	2	12
Pirates total	**246**	**1,498½**

Cyril Maurice James Squibb, known simply as Jim or Jimmy, first developed an interest in speedway way back in 1939, when he contacted Hackney Wick for a trial. However, the declaration of the Second World War put a halt to his ambitions when he instead joined up to do his bit for King and Country. After the hostilities, he bought a speedway bike in 1947, and having gained experience on the grass, he linked with Southampton.

Little did anyone know then, but he was to go on and become the club's all-time leading points-scorer in league racing. Anyway, such was his promise that he was invited to take part in the first post-war meeting at the Banister Court venue on 29 April, and he did well too, registering 10 points in an individual meeting for the Southampton Trophy. He proved to be a natural for the Saints and was to plunder 201½ points as he remained ever-present over the 28-match Third Division programme for the club. Such was the impression he made on management and supporters alike with his clever white-line riding, he was awarded the Charles Knott Trophy for being the leading first-year rider. Indeed, Jimmy won many points with a last-bend dash, and was certainly never beaten until the chequered flag dropped.

He went on to hit the jackpot in 1948, netting 375½ points from a full quota of 44 league meetings while also taking victory in a World Championship qualifying round at his home track. During the year he visited the newly-opened Poole for the first time on 17 May and, wearing the number one race-jacket, he simply burned up the cinders to establish a new track record of 81.0 seconds. The Pirates went on to win the league encounter 51-33 and Squibb finished with a tally of 11 points, only losing out on a maximum when beaten by home skipper Joe Bowkis in a pulsating heat 12.

When the Saints moved up to Division Two in 1949, he notched up another 303 league points, and when Bob Oakley left to join Wembley the following year, he was made club captain and celebrated by top-scoring with another 217 points.

The early 1950s were tough times for speedway, with tracks closing down in many areas; Southampton sadly went the way of so many others, after completing just 7 league matches in the 1951 campaign. At the time, Jimmy had recorded 57 points and although Poole showed a great interest in acquiring his signature, it was to First Division Harringay he went for the remainder of the season. However, the going wasn't easy in the highest sphere of British racing and at the end of the term, he had registered just 32 points from 13 league matches. The Racers were prepared to let him go at the end of the term, and although Wigan were keen to secure his services he plumped for home town club Poole, who in 1952 were embarking on their first season of Division Two activity.

Initially, Squibb occupied a reserve berth, and although that meant fewer rides he picked up useful 5-point tallies as the Pirates opened their league schedule with wins on the road at Liverpool (58-25) and Edinburgh (47-37). It wasn't long before he moved into the main body of the side, and as the season progressed Poole went from strength to strength, eventually landing the League Championship by an 8-point margin from nearest challengers Coventry. Showing he had put the disappointments of the previous year behind him, Jimmy appeared in every one of their 44 Second Division matches, scoring 253 points for a solid 7.64 average. It was clearly a case of the 'local boy made good' and the promotion indicated in their final programme of the year that he would be one of the mainstays in 1953. How right they were, as he plundered 217 points from a shortened league programme to occupy third spot in the team's scoring behind Ken Middleditch (292) and Terry Small (260). The Pirates ended the season as runners-up to Coventry, but everyone in the sport believed they would have retained their Championship had Brian Crutcher not been transferred to Wembley 10 matches into the campaign.

It was a case of déjà vu in the season that followed, with Bristol just edging the league title ahead of Poole – the West Country side having asked to drop down after enduring a torrid time in Division One. In a further repeat, Squibb was again third in the Pirates statistical run-down, having accrued 137½ points. After successive second-place finishes, the Dorseteers dominated the Second Division scene in 1955 and charged to the title ahead of Coventry. The side possessed no weak links and in an excellent season of racing Jimmy added another 186 league points to an ever-increasing career total.

Poole deservedly earned promotion to the First Division in 1956 but, Ken Middleditch and new signing Jack Biggs apart, the rest of the boys who had served the team so well over the years struggled to find form. The Pirates ended the year in sixth position out of the seven competing sides, with Squibb's contribution being 88 points from the 24-match league schedule for a 5.92 average.

The Poole bosses pulled out of league racing in 1957, leaving Jimmy initially without a track, before he eventually rejoined Southampton, whom Charles Knott had resurrected in 1952, and tallied 85 league points. Still with the Saints in 1958, he enjoyed a good year in the top-flight, posting a league average of 6.33 while also earning an England call-up to ride against Sweden in the first Test at Banister Court on 1 July. However, having begun the 1959 term with Southampton, he departed after a handful of matches and returned to Poole, who had reopened to league racing under the promotion of Vic Gooden a year previously. He went on to score 39 points from 8 league matches for the Pirates and it looked as though he was 'home'. This was not the case though, and thus Squibb began a period of wanderlust that saw him assist several clubs. Vic Gooden moved his assets to Ipswich in 1960 and the Dorset-born racer accompanied him to Foxhall Heath. He spent two years with the Witches, during which he totalled 145 points in National League circles. A move into the Provincial League followed in 1962, when he stormed to the head of Plymouth's scoring with 234 points. He then played a part in the revival of the sport at New Cross in 1963, and when the Old Kent Road venue again closed down in August, he was identified with Exeter. Jimmy was to stay with the Falcons right through until the end of the 1969 season, during which he was very consistent and totted up 1,469½ points in league racing alone.

Remarkably, at the age of forty-eight, he accepted a new challenge at Cradley Heath in 1970 and went on to supply the Black Country outfit with three years of solid service. He then dipped into the lower league with Eastbourne (1973) and Canterbury (1974-1975), before an injury finally convinced him to call it a day. After his retirement, he lived abroad for some years, but a period of indifferent health meant a return to 'the old country' in 2003. What a great servant to the sport he was from 1947 to 1975 inclusive, and it's a shame his efforts weren't rewarded with a benefit meeting.

Born: 18 September 1934, Poole, Dorset

Competition	Matches	Points
League	268	1,154½
National Trophy & Knock-Out Cup	35	126
Others	94	359
Three- and four-team tournaments	6	34
Pirates total	**403**	**1,673½**

Locally-born Norman Strachan might have been small in stature, but that didn't stop him from going on to become one of the Pirates' greatest servants. His bow at Wimborne Road came during the 1952 season; co-author Glynn Shailes has a programme recalling the events. The date was 9 June and that evening's meeting pitched Poole against Oxford in a National Trophy tie, with Norman programmed to ride in the second half. The Pirates had hammered the unfortunate Cheetahs by 78 points to 30 when he first appeared on track wearing a yellow and black helmet. Golden-voiced announcer Cliff R. Cooper helpfully informed everyone that the correct pronunciation of his name was 'Norman Strawn'. For a beginner, the youngster faced formidable opposition in the shape of Jimmy Squibb, Allan Kidd and Johnny Thomson. Small wonder that he came home last, although he was far from disgraced.

Poole went on to lift the Second Division Championship that year, while Norman continued to learn his trade with regular second-half outings. His progress was highlighted on 4 August, following a league match when Oxford again supplied the opposition and were slaughtered 68-16. The Cheetahs' highest scorers were their reserves Harry Saunders and Bill Osborne, with Strachan facing both in after-the-meeting events. In separate races, he beat the Oxford riders, while in the process also defeating the likes of Poole colleagues Allan Kidd, Johnny Thomson and Roy Craighead, all of whom were pretty nippy around the Wimborne Road raceway. In their end-of-season programme notes, promoters Len Matchan and Geoffrey Bravery described him as 'a rider who will make the grade in

speedway. Norman's riding in the second-half has caught the fancy of the crowd, who are always anxious to encourage him to greater success.'

In 1953, local hero Brian Crutcher was transferred to Wembley and the Pirates were pipped to the Division Two title by Coventry. Strachan was given team opportunities and although he only scored a total of 9 points from 5 league matches, there was much promise. More chances came his way in 1954, when Poole again had to settle for the runner-up spot in the Second Division behind Bristol. For a youngster amidst the hurly-burly of league racing, the recording of 43½ points was an excellent achievement and his efforts were recognised by speedway journalist Peter Morrish, who stated that 'Norman did well for a newcomer'.

Happily, he was a regular member of the Pirates side in 1955, when they carried all before them and raced to the Division Two

Championship. With Poole looking a power-house unit, a tally of 136 points from 29 league matches showed he had really played a part in the triumph. After such a good season personally, Strachan must have looked forward to even better things in 1956. However, the Pirates really became victims of their own success and found themselves promoted to the First Division, a league that was virtually dying on its feet. New riders were drafted in to strengthen the line-up and Poole did surprisingly well in the early part of the campaign, briefly heading the table at one stage. Opportunities were limited for Norman and it was a sharp learning curve, but nevertheless he still appeared in 11 league matches, netting 16 points for an average of 3.83.

It was a body blow in 1957 when Poole closed its doors to speedway and their team members were transferred elsewhere. Strachan took the opportunity of racing for Southampton, but only registered a single league point for the Saints. He did, however, get to ride for the Pirates after all, in a short series of open-licence meetings at Wimborne Road, run under the promotion of Jack Crutcher.

In 1958, Vic Gooden brought regular league racing back to Poole by relocating his Rayleigh outfit. Aside from the main National League competition, a Junior League was formed and Norman appeared in Poole's first such match when they entertained Swindon on 21 April. He tallied 11 points from 5 starts as his side collected a 31-28 victory, before going on to win the Junior Riders' Championship in the second half with a maximum 9 points. Officialdom then stepped in and decreed that as he had previously completed more than 6 matches for the senior team, he was barred from any further outings in the Junior League. It was a season of frustration for the rider, since he was only to represent the Pirates in 2 league matches, scoring but a single point. Nothing lasts for too long in speedway, however, and the following season, he not only raced for his beloved Poole, totalling 10 points, but also appeared for their second side in the National Reserve League, accumulating 29 points. Keeping himself busy, he was also identified in the Southern Area League with Aldershot, for whom he amassed 15 points.

The sport changed for the better in 1960, benefiting riders like Strachan who had lived for the day when there would be league racing they could enjoy without an ongoing struggle. The Provincial League was formed, with Poole, under the new promotion of Charles Knott Snr, becoming one of the ten competing sides. Norman jumped at the chance of a berth with the Pirates, and was joined by former team-mates Allan Kidd, Ken Middleditch and Tony Lewis, all of whom had missed the 1959 campaign for one reason or another. He quickly settled to the new sphere of racing and steadily went about the business of scoring 97 points from 16 league meetings. Among many good showings, perhaps his best was against a very strong Bristol outfit at Wimborne Road on 6 July, when Poole won a thrilling match 38-34. The diminutive rider won three races in fine style, but saw his chance of a full-house spoiled by Trevor Redmond in an exciting heat 8. In completing the match with 11 points, his super effort supported that of maximum man Ken Middleditch and played a vital part in the narrow victory.

Strachan was really enjoying his racing at this stage of his career – the Provincial League was tailor-made for him and he was a member of outstanding Poole sides which scooped back-to-back Championships in 1961 and 1962, having missed out by a whisker in 1960. In the former title-winning season, he notched 69 league points, while in 1962 he put together 130 points and especially enjoyed matches against Wolverhampton. Indeed, he followed up a 9-point tally versus the Midlanders at Wimborne Road on 30 May with a 10-point return from Monmore Green on 29 June. His most impressive performance, however, occurred in a home encounter against Newcastle on 8 August, when he scorched to a 12-point maximum.

It was another good year for the Pirates in 1963, and although they didn't make it three league titles in a row, they did fill third spot. With a total of 143 points, Norman was fourth in the club's list of league scorers, backing the heat-leaders all the way. The Provincial League operated outside the jurisdiction of the SCB in 1964, but Poole remained in place to occupy a mid-table position in the final analysis. Another 104 points flowed from the wheels of the wee man, and he also registered 23 points for Newpool (a composite team made up of Newport and Poole riders) in the uncompleted Metropolitan League.

With the birth of the British League in 1965, there was naturally an equalisation of team strengths and, although there were some changes in the Pirates ranks, Strachan once more began a season on board. He posted many useful scores, including a 4-ride paid maximum (11+1) against visiting Hackney on 12 May, and looked sharp in his racing until a bad shoulder injury curtailed his season in July. At the time he had recorded 89 points from 20 matches for a league average of 6.14. Fit again, he resumed with the Dorseteers in 1966 and, with competition keen for team places, he was always kept on his toes, although his league average did slip a tad to 5.41.

In 1967 he was to spend his final year with the side, prior to sampling pastures new. In a career that had seen him linked with Poole since 1952, he was ever-present throughout the 36-match league programme, scoring 175 points for an average of 5.78. Having had such a long association with the club, he would have been granted a Testimonial in modern times, but unluckily for him these things didn't happen in those days. It was to Newport that Norman pledged his future in 1968, remaining with the club for three full years before moving on again.

Although he began the 1971 season with a single league match for Wembley at Belle Vue, he soon relocated to Oxford, where he was mainly used at reserve until the end of 1972. Then, injury-hit Poole asked their former regular to help them out in 1973, having lost the services of four men before their first league match! Appearances were intermittent, with Norman being used as and when

required, but he did ride in 8 league matches, scoring a total of 16 points. Aside from assisting the Pirates, he also represented Coatbridge and dipped into the Second Division with Long Eaton.

That still wasn't the last the speedway world had seen of him, since he came out of retirement in September 1974, riding for Coatbridge in a Knock-Out Cup fixture at Eastbourne and a league match at Canterbury before finally hanging up his leathers for good. These days he seldom misses a meeting at Poole, and always greets everyone with a smile and a firm handshake. In the long and proud history of the club, he was undoubtedly one its most loyal riders.

Born: 1928, Ballornock, Glasgow

Competition	Matches	Points
League	57	203
National Trophy	14	94
Others	40	131
Pirates total	**111**	**428**

Scottish-born John K. Thomson lived and worked in Witchampton, Dorset, and an early speedway story said that legendary promoter Johnnie Hoskins made an approach for the freckle-faced youngster, claiming that a Scotsman riding for his Ashfield outfit was just what he needed. Thomson was always interested in 'things mechanical' and was a regular competitor on the local grass-track circuits. Away from racing, his job was that of a maintenance mechanic, working on vehicles at the premises of Witchampton Paper Mills, where his father was also an employee.

Johnny linked with Poole in 1951, and, with team places at a premium, he was initially restricted to second-half events. A window of opportunity opened in a competition entitled the Festival of Britain Trophy, which was run with ten-man teams, and he grasped his chance with both hands, making his debut in the first such match at home to Plymouth on 9 April. The Pirates always held the upper hand and raced to a massive 74-46 victory, with Johnny enjoying an excellent meeting to garner 5 points. However, although he went on to appear in all 8 of Poole's matches in the Festival of Britain Trophy, scoring a total of 24 points, he was to only represent the side in 3 challenge fixtures throughout the rest of the season. Still, he plugged away in the second

halves and was even the surprise recipient of an England cap at 'C' level on 6 September, when the Wimborne Road raceway played host to a Test match against the USA. Thomson arrived merely to spectate, but, with Bob Roger being a non-arrival, he was immediately dispatched back home to fetch his bike and leathers so as to take the place of the Exeter rider and officially line up as second reserve. In the event he didn't get a ride, as England slipped to a 62-46 defeat on a rain-soaked track, with the Poole promotion subsequently commenting that 'in the circumstances it would not have been fair to him or his colleagues to have used him'.

Having won the Division Three Championship, the Pirates deservedly earned promotion, and Johnny again found it hard to claim a team berth in 1952. Despite this, he seemed content to remain on the books and was always happy to fill in as and when required. An example of this occurred in May, when Ken Middleditch had a spell on the sidelines through injury. The young Glaswegian was called up to replace his skipper for 4 matches, and actually made his league debut at Leicester on 2 May, netting a single point in a 49-35 loss. All told, he made 7 league appearances during the year, recording 21 points for a 6.67 average. It was clear that he could have walked into almost any other team in the Southern League (formerly the Third Division), but Thomson's loyalty to Poole finally paid off in 1953, when he was handed a team spot.

The Pirates were considerably weakened when Brian Crutcher was transferred to Wembley after 10 league matches, but they still managed to finish the campaign in second place, just a point behind Champions Coventry. Johnny held his place throughout the 32-match league programme to record

82 points, his best performance being a tally of 8 in a 42-42 draw at Stoke on 13 June.

In 1954, Bristol opted to drop down a league from the First Division to the Second, and a battle royal took place between the Pirates and the Bulldogs for the Championship, with Swindon also very much in contention. The title eventually went the way of Bristol, with Poole again having to settle for the runner-up position, and Thomson's contribution to the cause was 67 points from 13 matches. For a second year running, his best showing occurred on the road, when he accrued 9 points at Southampton on 20 July.

The 1955 season came along and it looked like being the year when he would finally realise his great potential with the Pirates. He certainly showed signs of this in a league encounter at Swindon on 16 April when, after a couple of third-place finishes, he accompanied Ken Middleditch to a 5-1 over Ian Williams and Ron Swaine in heat 11 . Later, in heat 14, he raced away to win ahead of partner Bill Holden, the duos maximum giving Poole a 6-point lead with 2 races remaining. The Dorseteers went on to secure a 49-47 victory and, credited with 9+2 points, Johnny Thomson was undoubtedly the hero of the hour. Among other good showings, he was to hit scores of 15 points away at Rayleigh in a National Trophy tie on 23 April and 13 points at home to Leicester in a league fixture two days later. He was definitely on the up, but then tragedy struck in a National Trophy match at home to Ipswich on 9 May. He already had 2 points to his name when he crashed badly in heat 9 and was taken to Poole General Hospital with a fractured left femur. Sadly, he suffered an embolism and passed away four days later. It was a terrible shock, not just to his family and friends, but to all speedway supporters the length and breadth of Britain.

Johnny's funeral took place on 16 May, exactly one week after the track accident, with members of the Poole team acting as bearers of his coffin. His death badly hit brothers Frank and Doug Holcombe, who had backed and supported him over the years, so much so that they donated a Memorial Cup, which was presented later that year, to Bill Holden on 11 July. A Memorial Shield was subsequently paid for by

the supporters and, whether as a second-half event or a full-blown meeting, was raced for at Poole from 1955-1973 inclusive. Interestingly, a memorial event was also staged for Johnny at Rye House on 13 May 1956, when Eric Hockaday came out on top in a meeting contested by riders from the Southern Area League.

JOHNNY THOMSON MEMORIAL SHIELD ROLL OF HONOUR

1955   Allan Kidd
1956   Cyril Roger
1957   Brian Crutcher
1958   Ken McKinlay
1959   Ron How
1960   Tony Lewis
1961   Jack Scott
1962   Geoff Mudge
1963   Ross Gilbertson
1964   Jimmy Squibb
1965   Bill Andrew
1966   Bill Andrew
1967   Reidar Eide
1968   Barry Briggs
1969   Geoff Mudge
1970   Trevor Hedge
1971   Pete Smith
1972   Pete Smith
1973   Bernt Persson

Born: 24 November 1953, Salisbury, Wiltshire

Competition	Matches	Points
League	245	1,337
Knock-Out Cup	20	88
Others	59	330
Three- and four-team tournaments	28	147
Pirates total	**352**	**1,902**

Martin Yeates had an interest in bikes from an early age, and having nagged his aunt and uncle into taking him along, he first saw speedway at Swindon as an eight-year-old. In his teens he often bunked off school, preferring to mess around on bikes, and eventually moved onto grass-track racing, where he was spotted by Poole rider Brian Collins, who suggested he gave speedway a try. Following a few practice laps at Matchams Park in 1971, Martin made such rapid strides that he broke into the Poole side the following season, riding in 3 league matches.

In 1973, he made several appearances alongside then rider/coach Mike Broadbanks for Chesterton in the Second Division (later to become Stoke). He also again rode for Poole when required, as well as furthering his experience at Division Two level with Eastbourne. The management at the East Sussex track were suitably impressed and he was to spend 1974 in the Eagles' colours. In spite of his inexperience, Yeates seemed to take everything in his stride, achieving a creditable 6-point average, while also 'doubling-up' for Poole in 11 First Division meetings. There was also an outing for Oxford, and although this didn't yield any points, within three years he was to become very much the 'King of Cowley' at the university venue. Prior to that, and in a move closer

to home, he was to link with Weymouth in 1975, and it was while at the Dorset club that he became a leading light in the retitled National League. He finely tuned his starting technique and acquired the nickname of 'Trapper', plundering 299 points from 35 matches for a league average of 8.05.

Having become a heat-leader, Martin increased his league average to 8.52 with the then-nicknamed Wizards in 1976, but it was with Oxford a year later that he really hit the heights. Tall scoring became the routine and from 35 league matches, he accumulated a total of 396 points for a massive 10.59 average. Such was his exceptional form that only Tom Owen (11.00) and Colin Richardson (10.70) finished above him in the entire National League averages. Yeates had also continued to race for parent club Poole as and when needed throughout his time with both Weymouth and Oxford. One performance that particularly stood out occurred at Wimborne Road on 28 September 1977, when he raced to a paid full-house (11+1) in a league match against Bristol.

Given his record with the Cheetahs, it came as little surprise when the Pirates wanted him on a full-time basis in 1978. Obviously the going was a lot tougher, but he did exceptionally well to net 174 points for an average of 6.08 from 35 British League matches. Those admirable figures included another super 4-ride paid maximum (11+1), which was registered when Sheffield visited Poole on 11 August. Unfortunately, having done so well, the 1979 campaign was to prove a confidence-sapping experience, and with a tally of 105 points in league racing, his average slumped to 4.36.

Although he did ride in several meetings for Poole in 1980, Martin was happy to settle back into a consistent high-scoring groove with Weymouth in the National League, posting a season's total of 375 points for an average of 9.23. During the year, he also appeared in a couple of British League matches for Swindon, the first being a home encounter versus King's Lynn on 11 July, when he notched a 3-point tally.

He enjoyed another splendid season with Weymouth in 1981, raising his league average to 9.97, while also again linking with Swindon as an old-fashioned number eight. Yeates did well for the Robins too, making 9 league appearances for a 5.29 average in his inimitable leaning style. In a similar vein, he continued to represent Weymouth and Swindon in 1982 and 1983, making more than useful contributions to the Robins' cause on many occasions. In a sport famous for rumours, various stories suggested he had been transferred to Swindon, but it isn't certain if any fee actually changed hands. However, being very popular with supporters at the Wiltshire track, Martin decided to give the top league his full attention once more in 1984, but regrettably the move didn't really work out for rider or club. He only managed to attain a 3.73 average from 9 League Cup matches, and after completing 2 league meetings he again returned to Weymouth. The amazing thing was that he might lose out to a reserve or back-up rider, only to then have the skill and daring to go out and soundly beat the opposition's number one! This happened a number of times during Richard Vowles' reign as promoter of the Robins, a fact which really puzzled the Swindon boss.

Having rejoined Weymouth, Yeates straight away slipped back into a high-scoring groove to post an average 10.35 and finish just behind Glasgow's Steve Lawson (10.40) in the overall National League figures. A personal highlight occurred that year when he finished fifth in the British Final at a rain-soaked Coventry on 20 June, his performance including a memorable victory over eventual winner Kenny Carter. Although he bowed out of the World Championship in the Overseas Final, it was still a tremendous achievement, for he became the first rider from the National League to progress so far.

Weymouth promoters Mervyn Stewkesbury and Pete Ansell moved their operation along the South Coast to Wimborne Road in 1985, and Martin was more than happy to skipper the retitled Poole Wildcats. He was a fine captain too, and notched 294 points from 35 matches, with no less than 10 maximums coming his way (8 full and 2 paid). Solidly averaging 8.62, he finished third in the side's pecking order, his efforts efficiently backing those of fellow heat-leaders Stan Bear (9.89) and Kevin Smith (9.38), as the Dorseteers were just pipped to the league title by Ellesmere Port.

Remaining on board in 1986, Yeates continued to lead his charges by example, recording 348 league points for an average of 8.80. Again, he occupied third spot in the club's statistical breakdown, behind Steve Schofield (10.45) and Kevin Smith (9.36), with the Wildcats once more having to settle for the runner-up position in the league table, behind Eastbourne.

In 1987, 'Trapper' announced it would be his final fling in the saddle, and with Poole reverting back to their traditional Pirates nickname, he remained ever-present throughout the 30-match league programme to notch 252 points for an 8.03 average. He enjoyed a farewell meeting at Wimborne Road on 20 October, when the Superstars beat the Megastars 42-36, the highlight on a rain-soaked track being the defeat of Hans Nielsen by Poole favourite David Biles. It was fitting that in the last meeting of the season at Poole a week later, on 27 October, Martin ended his career on a winning note, when he and partner Jonathan Blake raced to victory in the Travis & Arnold Best Pairs. Despite never winning it, Yeates was one of the most successful competitors in the National League Riders' Championship, twice grabbing second place (1977 and 1980) and also finishing third on two occasions (1983 and 1984). In 1993, Martin returned to Swindon as an astute team manager, prior to joining forces with partner Peter Toogood to take over the promoting licence in 1995. The duo remained in the hotseat for 1996, but pressure of outside business caused Yeates to stand down at the end of the season, with Peter Toogood assuming full control of the club.

Other related titles published by Tempus:

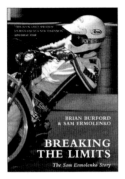

Breaking the Limits The Sam Ermolenko Story
BRIAN BURFORD & SAM ERMOLENKO

After a horrific road accident in his native sunny California left him virtually unable to walk, it took Sam Ermolenko an awful lot of bravery and determination to make a recovery – let alone become a speedway world champion! Despite a late start in the sport and a further series of severe injuries, Sam has overcome all the odds and reached the very top. This is his remarkable story.
0 7524 3225 7

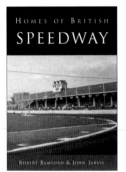

Homes of British Speedway
ROBERT BAMFORD & JOHN JARVIS

This ambitious and comprehensive work features over 300 speedway venues around Britain, affording each track statistical information including address, years of operation, track lengths, promoters and club successes. The more important homes of speedway, for example Belle Vue, Swindon, Wimbledon and Coventry, all receive highly detailed synopses.
0 7524 2210 3

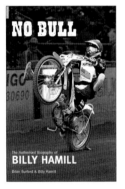

No Bull The Authorised Biography of Billy Hamill
BRIAN BURFORD & BILLY HAMILL

In 1996, in a dramatic final race of the World Championship series, Billy Hamill became the fourth American to win the sport's top individual prize. *No Bull* is the compelling biography of the man they called 'the Bullet', in which Billy gives his frank, honest and sometimes heart-breaking views of his struggle to make it to the top.
0 7524 3219

Speedway Through the Lens of Mike Patrick
MIKE PATRICK

A familiar figure to anyone who is interested in speedway, Mike Patrick goes further than any other photographer to get the most original and impressive shots. This is a selection of his finest images, featuring famous riders at work and at play, amazing action shots and important speedway moments.
0 7524 2596 X

If you are interested in purchasing other books published by Tempus, or in case you have difficulty finding any Tempus books in your local bookshop, you can also place orders directly through our website

www.tempus-publishing.com